GET YOUR MOVE ON

TEFO KHAMA

GET YOUR MOVE ON

Get Your Move On
First Edition,
First Impression 2020
ISBN 978-1-990961-45-8

Published by:
Inspired Publishing
PO Box 82058 | Southdale | 2135
Johannesburg, South Africa
Email: info@inspiredpublishing.co.za
www.inspiredpublishing.co.za

CONTENTS

Dedication		1
Acknowledgements		2
Preface		6
Introduction		10
Chapter One	The Big Divide: Movement Vs Stagnation	14
Chapter Two	Life And Death - Movement And Stagnation	28
Chapter Three	Life And Death In Many Shapes And Sizes	48
Chapter Four	Move Stoppers	72
Chapter Five	Inspirational Life Moves – Recent History	90
Chapter Six	On The Move? Expect Opposition!	140
Chapter Seven	How To Get Your Move On!	165

DEDICATION

To my wife Kelebogile Khama, a true good gift and my personal favour from the Lord. Thank you for all the support, the friendship, the companionship, the laughter, the highs and the lows. Thank you for always saying to me: “don’t worry babe, you got this!” Most importantly I am grateful to you for believing in our love and for loving me. I love you Madloks!

To my children Oratiloe, Atang, Khaphatseho and Thoriso; believe in God so that you can believe in the dreams He has deposited in your hearts. Always remember that you must run your own race and leave your own footprints on this earth. You have my love and support always. Never remain in stagnation, always get your move on!

To my late mother Mme Dimakatso Khama, and my father Ntate Fusi Khama; look at what God has done through your son. I can safely say “I know you are proud”.

ACKNOWLEDGEMENTS

I give all the honour, majesty, splendor and glory to God the Father; the Son Jesus Christ - my Lord and Saviour; and The Holy Spirit - my Comforter, Counselor and Teacher. I am a testimony of Your grace, and I am truly blessed to be Your servant and vessel in my generation. May I decrease and may You increase!

Thank you to my wife Kelebogile, for reminding me always that I must press on and complete everything that I commit to. I have got your back. Your private sacrifices are now displayed as our public success. I love and appreciate you, always! My children; I love you. Destiny is calling you; pursue it with passion and faith in Christ Jesus!

To my late mother Mme Dimakatso, I will always have fond and beautiful memories of you. Your unique and heartwarming laughter remains unforgettable, and it carried me through my childhood; I will always love you. To my stepmother Mme Eunice, thank you for helping my father to raise us. I can only imagine how tough it was; with hindsight, your entrepreneurial spirit was something special; the lessons are not lost. To my father Ntate Fusi, thank you for encouraging me to read and for sacrificing for us (your children) to go to school. You were not able to go far in your schooling due to lack of opportunities in your era, but you desired for all your children to get educated and have meaningful lives. Your seed cannot fail; it will continue to bear fruit even to future generations.

We will continue to look up to you, O sebeditse Mokoena Oa Monaheng, re a leboha!

To my spiritual parents, Pastor Phathisizwe and Mama Nomsa Gubevu, thank you for welcoming me and my family into your family. I will continue to learn from your love for the Lord and your dedication to His Kingdom. Thank you for saying: "You need the Son", and that was my miracle, look at the fruit! May God bless you exceedingly abundantly.

To Prophet Lebogang and Pastor Phumzile Mashigo, I will not be able to express my love and gratitude with words. May God answer all your prayers and enlarge your territory. I see that global ministry, "eye has not seen, ear has not heard, neither has it entered the heart"... all the things that God has prepared for you.

To Pastor Tinashe "Muendamberi" and Mama Regina Muzanarwo; I look at your life in Christ and I see a demonstration of carrying the cross daily and following Jesus Christ. You are a rare breed and an inspiration in our generation. May God open doors for you on earth and in Heaven, and may you walk in abundance from His good treasures.

A special word of gratitude to Pastor Thamsanqa and Mama Sunshine Mathiso, as well as Reverend Witness and Pastor Tsholo Acts. Thank you for always being there for me and my family right from the beginning. I am always thankful for your prayers, support and counsel. May God lift up His countenance upon you.

To the Khama and Lechakane families, my siblings, cousins, uncles, aunts, nieces, nephews and extended family; thank you for being there throughout my journey, I love and appreciate you. To my in-laws, the Ngema, Moduka, Mallela, Molefe, Chele and Tsomane families; thank you for welcoming me, showing me love and treating me as a son; may God bless you all.

A special message of gratitude to the leadership and membership of Mt Zion Assembly of the Apostolic Faith Mission (AFM) in Vosloorus; what a home my family has found. Thank you for the warmth, the support and the love; may favour be your portion.

To my family in the Lord in all assemblies and ministries, destiny helpers, my prayer partners, brothers, sisters, coaches, mentors, friends, associates, superiors and colleagues; thank you for your contributions and for being a great part of my life. Sincere apologies that I am not able to list all of you; may God bless you all beyond your expectations.

A hearty and special word of gratitude to my publisher - Inspired Publishing. Darren August and the dream team; you are legends; many will soon agree. Look at your work! God will never forget your labour of love.

In addition to the authors and sources referenced and cited in this book, I would like to acknowledge the contribution of preachers, teachers, speakers and authors that have impacted my thinking and way of life, as well as your collective influence to the content of this book.

To all the readers of this book and attendees of our workshops and training; if it were not for you, this book would be worthless. Thank you for the love and support. May God bless you all!

PREFACE

Life is movement, and stagnation is death. Creation demonstrates this fact in many shapes and forms, from conception of a new life, to the first kick, to the movement into the outside world through birth. Animals migrate, hibernate, and move out of hibernation in order to preserve life and ensure the survival of their species. The rivers flow and bring and sustain lives and livelihoods along their path.

When God created the heavens and the earth, He said: “Let there be light…” and this was the first movement in our universe when light appeared and darkness disappeared. Ever since creation, the universe keeps moving, and planets continue to orbit in the galactic world; with our own planet earth sustaining life by moving at a breathtaking 108 000km/h around the Sun. God created man, both male and female, and they were mobile and were given the assignment to be fruitful and multiply; a commandment for progress, which is another form of movement.

When Jesus Christ came to the pool of Bethesda, he encountered the lame man who was waiting with others for an angel to come stir (and move) the water in the pool. The man had been stuck on his bed for 38 years because of his infirmity which restricted his movement. Because of his limitations which resulted in lack of speed, this man could not make his way into the water, as each time the water was stirred someone quicker would beat him to it. The infirmity of the man touched Jesus' heart and He asked the man if he would like to be made whole; and afterwards commanded him to take up his bed and walk. When Peter and John came to the temple, they also encountered a man who was lame, and he was sitting and begging at the gate called Beautiful. They realised that money was not going to help this man, and the only permanent solution was to introduce this man to movement. They commanded him to rise and walk in the name of Jesus. These two examples from the Scriptures demonstrate the importance of movement; and this is not limited to physical movement, but freedom to move from physical, mental, spiritual, career, business, relational and all other forms of stagnation.

It is inevitable that all of us at one point or another will find ourselves in a place of stagnation. We must however always remember that this should never be our permanent residence. We can all accidentally stumble into stagnation, but it will take a conscious and decisive choice to break free, step forth and get our move on. Our choices will determine the eventual outcome of either death in stagnation or life through movement; and that is why the Bible says: “I have set before you life and death... now choose life, that you and your descendants may live…” History and Biblical history provide us with ample evidence of people and movements who continue to capture our collective imagination; because they refused to stay in stagnation, but they rather chose to start moving and kept moving, and were able, as a result, to change the course of history.

This book provides examples from the natural world, the world of work, industries, government, economies, religion, politics, social formations, individuals and societies, on the importance of movement and the need to make the right move at the appropriate times for self-sustenance and preservation. There are careers that have ended because they failed to move with the times. There are industries that have either disappeared or have lost their prestige and stature due to lack of movement. Some companies had to file for bankruptcy and close shop all because of failure to read the tide and move accordingly. There are men and women whom history continues to judge harshly, because they failed to move in the right pace and rhythm of the changes in their societies.

It is not necessarily easy for us humans to embrace change, and this makes us prone to falling victims to move stoppers such as fear, anxiety, uncertainties, lack of resources or support, and a myriad of other factors. In addition, all movements will encounter some form of opposition, and often; the greater the move, the greater the opposition it will face. We have to always recognise that there is no great achievement that can spring forth from a place of permanent stagnation. We must remember that greater glory lies ahead and it cannot be apprehended while we are stuck in the past. We must make a decision that we will not remain stuck, and we must derive a plan to move and make the necessary sacrifices in order for us to advance towards a brighter future with better prospects. Our faith in God must always guide our decisions and actions, and it must be the foundation for all our moves. Remember that your move will impact and inspire others, and it will also be a foundation for all your future moves.

It is my hope and prayer that this book will ignite in you that fire which you need to propel you forward into a glorious future. Life is called a journey, and a journey is only useful to those who are willing to travel.

It is time to rise and get your move on, your life might just depend on it! Tefo Khama, Johannesburg, South Africa, November 2020

INTRODUCTION

"Life is like riding a bicycle, to keep your balance, you must keep moving." - Albert Einstein

Movement is one of the sure signs of life and this is seen in plants, animals, and humanity. The universe itself is alive, hence the movement of one planet around another in the form of galactic orbits. Even without technologies such as sonar, and other medical probes, and equipment, the movement of a baby in the womb of its mother is a sign of life, while lack of motion is always worrying and causes despair. It is for this reason that one of the most thrilling human experiences is to feel a child move for the first time in the womb, and I can only imagine how magical this experience is to an expectant mother.

The Nile river, which is reputed to be the longest river in the world, has its source in the Great Lakes region of Central Africa in Tanzania, and it snakes through nine countries, on a journey of more than 6500km until it empties itself into the Mediterranean Sea in Egypt. The most remarkable thing about this river is the life it gives as its waters move through these territories. This river has contributed significantly, perhaps more than any other force of nature, to the development of Egypt from ancient times to the present day. The Nile continues to sustain lives and livelihood, because it is not stagnant.

Every year gazelles, zebras, and wildebeest (1, 5 million strong herd) have to move between the Serengeti in Tanzania and the Masai Mara in Kenya. This movement is known as the Great Migration of the Serengeti; it is a migration of such magnitude that it is one of the ten wonders of the natural world. The migration continues to draw keen interest and attract visitors and it remains one of the most interesting areas of study in the natural sciences, all because the animals did not stay stagnant.

The primary purpose of this great movement is to avoid death; those animals that remain behind for whatever reason die in their place of stagnation. The same tragic fate awaits those animals that fail to move and make the journey to the destination. Perhaps the biggest tragedy befalls animals that begin the trek, yet due to lack of movement - be it intentional or accidental - find themselves falling victims to a stampede and dying on the journey. They meet their demise because of failure to move in the right direction and at the right pace.

Some animals make a move and fall prey to lions, crocodiles, leopards and other predators, because they take wrong steps.

Animals that keep moving tenaciously towards the intended destination eventually arrive in the land of lush pastures and abundant water.

The Bible records the greatest movement of people in the book of Exodus, when the children of Israel left the land of slavery in Egypt to journey through the wilderness before entering the promised land of Canaan. Some of the Israelites failed to make it to the Promised Land because their hearts and minds remained in the land of slavery, hence their rebellion against Moses and God, and sadly, they perished in the wilderness. Those who perished in the wilderness never truly moved out of Egypt, their minds and attitudes remained stagnant even in the midst of the greatest move on earth.

Deuteronomy 30:19 says, "This day I call the heavens and the earth as witnesses against you that I have set before you life and death, blessings and curses. Now choose life, so that you and your children may live." Each one of us has a choice to make, and what we choose may lead to life or death, and this life or death is in all areas of our lives. The choice you make determines the eventual outcome, so if you stay long enough on a train track, a train might come along and end your life, so refuse stagnation and avoid premature death.

CHAPTER ONE

THE BIG DIVIDE: MOVEMENT VS STAGNATION

"There are many ways of going forward, but only
One way of standing still." - Franklin d. Roosevelt

In the introduction we learned that life is best epitomised in and through movement. Survival is inherently dependent on making the right movement at the right time. The dictionary definition of movement reads: "an act of moving" or "a change or development". Stagnation is "a state of not flowing or moving" and "lack of activity, growth, or development". It is clear that stagnation is an absence of movement, and perhaps this is stating the obvious, but this contrast is very important to note and acknowledge, as this awareness is critical in how we view, justify, and promote stagnation.

Some of the synonyms for movement are progress, effort, advancement, development, growth, drive, leap, and activity. A few synonyms of stagnation are inactivity, stuck, inertia, immobility, sluggishness, and unproductivity, to name a few. Stagnation and immobility jeopardises our survival in various areas of life.

If a dangerous land animal is chasing you, you can jump into a river for your safety; however, you cannot stay in the river indefinitely as you may expose yourself to the danger of being swept away or overstaying may make you vulnerable to aquatic monsters. Someone once said if you and a few people are in the wild, ensure you have someone whom you can outrun. When the wild animals attack, all you need to do is to keep running (moving) and ensure that you are not last in the fleeing pack.

Movement can take many forms. A child in the womb must continually move in order to exercise, grow, and develop; however, more importantly, the child moves to stay alive and the movement also serves as assurance that the child is still alive. A child in the womb must not be stagnant, so lack of movement is a cause for fear and panic for any pregnant mother.

A car that moves, no matter how slow, eventually gets you to your destination. There is a common saying that “better late than never"; if you keep moving you may arrive late, but you will surely arrive. If you want to never arrive, stay stagnant.

We can see some of the everyday contrasts between movement and stagnation in the following examples and all of us at one point or another face these situations:

◆ EXERCISE AND INACTIVITY

There are people who exercise, and people who wish they could exercise, but for various reasons are not able to, and then there are people who have no interest nor intention to exercise. People who like or even love exercise will always find a reason to be active; they would use every opportunity from everyday activities or chores and incorporate them into some form of workout. On the other hand, those who hate exercise will find all reasons to avoid any form of activity. Some of the contrasting attitudes that are adopted by the two types of people are shown below:

◆ Stairs Or Not

At any given opportunity, active people would gladly take the stairs instead of using the escalator or elevator. Every time a person who has this attitude faces a choice between stairs and an easier and more convenient alternative, their answer is always an instinctive: "stairs it is!"

The shunner of exercise will avoid the stairs if there is an easier option. Such a person sees absolutely nothing wrong with waiting a good five to ten minutes for an elevator, and it matters little if the person is going up or downstairs, the attitude remains consistent; it is “stairs: not a chance!”.

◆ Chores

There are people who avoid chores or errands that involve physical activity; if they have an option to pay someone to do the chores then they would take it. If there are no means to outsource labour for the chores, they burden other family members, such as spouses or children.

Those who love performing chores have an attitude that says any chore or errand is a welcome activity to stretch, stay active, and do something different. They view errands as an opportunity to see new things and to appreciate the joys of being able to move around.

◆ Keeping Fit

Someone once said, “You cannot inherit a six-pack ab by merely gazing continually at a picture of one.” There are people who like to keep fit and they make time and effort to work on their fitness, and they will train beyond the pain barrier as they put miles on the road, extra weights on the bench, cycle until they run out of sweat, read up and try every new training concept that they come across.

Some of us would go to great lengths to avoid working on our fitness; we would even have innovative and skillful ways to side step (no pun intended) any opportunity to risk moving our fitness even a notch. The most famous words for this group of people are: "Next year I want to start the year properly and kick start it with a killer fitness programme." Some would even go as far as purchasing a new training gear, complete with colourful and fashionable training shoes. There are those who are brazen in their anti-fitness campaign, they do not even care to feign a desire to work out; instead, their favourite line is: "We are all going to die one day so why bother." Just because we are going to die someday does not mean we must neglect our bodies, which the Bible calls the Temple of God.

◆ BOREDOM AND CREATIVITY

There is a foreign concept (to me at least) called boredom. This is a dullness of heart and mind, which leads to one feeling uninterested in anything, and a perception that life is offering nothing meaningful, let alone exciting.

Boredom begins with inactivity, not just physical inactivity, but more importantly, the inactivity of the mind. An idle mind is a mind in stagnation and that is why it breeds boredom, which fuels a lack of interest in life in general, and if this continues, it can lead to dysfunctional habits, which lead to a dysfunctional life. Therefore, a dysfunctional life is an enemy of progress and derails a destiny.

It is impossible for a creative mind to suffer from boredom. God created a mind to create; that is why creativity is one of the best ways to keep the mind young, fresh, and productive. A creative mind will never suffer boredom, just as a wise man will not suffer fools.

In order for our minds to remain active and creative, we need to keep our mental faculties continually engaged and stimulated in a meaningful and positive way; we can do this through reading, watching shows, partaking in games, writing, thinking innovatively, developing creative ideas, learning new skills, studying, listening, and speaking.

The key is to keep our creative juices flowing and our minds creatively active through positive and impactful stimuli. For example, there are people who read, but they only read gossip columns; it is good that they do read, but the content of what they read is not meaningful nor useful; it is a way of killing time. Learning a new skill keeps the mind fresh, engaged, and developing, and it has motivational benefits.

◆ COMPLAINING AND "SOLUTIONING"

Complaining is one of the easiest sports that any person can partake in; it does not require any skill or talent. The tools for complaining are a mind, a mouth, and an attitude of pessimism and fault-finding. As easy as complaining might be, and how often harmless it may appear to be, this is one of the surest ways to fail in life. Numbers 11:1 says, "The people began to complain to the Lord about their troubles. When the

Lord heard them, he became angry and sent fire on the people. It burned among them and destroyed one end of the camp."

From this passage of scripture, we see the fire of God consuming some of the children of Israel for their penchant for complaining. For some reason they appear to have not learned their lesson, as many of them eventually missed out on entering and possessing the promised land because of complaining and murmuring. God has good plans for us, but we can complain ourselves out of His noble plans. The strange thing with us humans is that when we invite failure because of our complaints, instead of owning up, we add salt to the wound by blaming others or even God for our self-inflicted wounds.

God Has Good Plans For Us, But We Can Complain Ourselves Out Of His Noble Plans.

"Solutioning" is definitely a bad grammar word; however, it is the greatest antidote to "complaining". Complaining does not offer solutions, thus people who want to achieve something meaningful in life shun those who complain. Instead of complaining, solutioning sees the trouble or problem as an opportunity to generate new solutions. If the attitude of the Israelites in the wilderness was for solutioning, then they would have used their troubles to understand God and His ways better.

It is often in the midst of trouble that our faith is tested, and if we pass the test, great testimonies result from what seemed to be an insurmountable mountain. A murmurer sees a mountain as an insurmountable obstacle, while the solutionist sees a mountain as an opportunity to climb higher and see new opportunities beyond it. A solutionist thrives in the midst of trouble, problems, obstacles, and opposition.

◆ WORK AND LAZINESS

Excessive reasoning often hides laziness; a lazy person would invest time in finding intelligent-sounding reasons for why they cannot do something. If the sluggard cannot find a reason to get out of a task, he

GET YOUR MOVE ON would resort to procrastination, knowing that if something is deferred to a future date, the future can remain in the future for as long as it serves the interests of the sluggard. The book of Proverbs is rich in wisdom and two passages of scripture that deal with laziness are nothing short of gems or pearls of wisdom, and these are stated below:

Proverbs 26:15 presents an award-winning level of laziness; it says, "Lazy people are too lazy to lift the food from their plate to their mouth." This is beyond comprehension, even when food is placed in front of him, a lazy person can starve to death. Many people have been given great opportunities, however due to laziness they shunned or ignored those prospects because they involved too much work.

Proverbs 20:4 says, "Some people are too lazy to plant seeds. So at harvest time, they look for food and find nothing." This is an attitude of a lazy person who expects to be rewarded for laziness, an impossibility of impossibilities.

Proverbs 22:13 says, "A person who is lazy and wants to stay home says, "There is a lion outside, and I might be killed in the streets!" Just when you think you have heard all excuses, and this one floors you. Laziness can make a person creative with excuses; however, no positive result could ever accrue from lazy hands. Laziness is free yet costly.

The word "work" is scary for lazy people. However, everything that has been built by humans since the beginning of time involved some form of work. There is nothing called "lowly work" and that is why God says in Deuteronomy 28:12, the Lord will "...bless all the work of your hand." In Colossians 3:23, we learn that "And whatever you do, do it heartily, as for the Lord and not for men." Therefore, the blessing is not dependent on the nature of the work, only a lazy hand cannot be blessed. It is therefore not a coincidence that before God gave any other instruction to Man at Creation, He assigned him to work in the Garden of Eden, because work produces and replenishes.

If there is no work in the form of employment, start with what appears to be a hobby, or take opportunities to volunteer or create work by starting a small business. Many have stumbled into greatness through such, hence the Bible says do not despise the day of small beginnings. Start working where you are and with what you have, remember God said to

Moses, "what is that in your hand?"

◆ DEMORALISED AND MOTIVATED

To be demoralised is another form of stagnation, because there is very little, if any, progress in one's thought process and actions under this condition. When you are demoralised or demotivated even the smallest or easiest tasks seems gargantuan and impossible. A demoralised person has the potential to draw others into that state, as we know the saying: "misery loves company." The people that we hang around and what we expose ourselves to continually can worsen and prolong the state of demoralisation, no wonder Paul warns in 1 Corinthians 15:33: "Don't let anyone fool you...bad companions make a good person bad." The longer one stays stuck in demotivation, the worse it may get and the more the future is threatened as the state of demotivation can deepen and eventually spiral out of control if there is no timely intervention. A negative attitude towards life will contribute to a state of continuous demoralisation.

Motivated effort trumps talent, especially if the talented person is demotivated. Motivation drives a person to seek more, dream more, desire more, aim for improvement, and better results. A motivated person sees mountains as obstacles to conquer. Motivation breeds a mindset that always thrives in difficult times, because challenges are opportunities to explore new ways of thinking and doing. A motivated person is a person who stays on the move, that is why "movers and shakers" are generally people who are highly motivated.

The best way to get motivated is to continually encourage ourselves through the Word of God. In the Bible, we see this in 1 Samuel 30 when the Amalekites had ransacked and plundered Ziklag, and taken the wives and children captive. David and his men cried until they had no strength to cry anymore, and the men planned to stone him as they blamed him for the misfortune, but the Bible says, "David encouraged himself in the Lord his God" and because of this, God spoke and they pursued the Amalekites and recovered more than they had lost. The Bible has more than enough material to motivate us even in the direst of situations.

◆ PROGRESSIVE OR BACKWARD

There are situations in life that can set one back; there are decisions that we make that can take us backwards in life. However, it is more detrimental to have a mindset that is fixed on the past and this mindset is best revealed in statements like "we miss the good old days". In the book of Judges 6, Gideon suffered from this type of mindset before the encounter with the angel of God. We hear him speaking nostalgically about the God of yesterday who parted the sea and performed great miracles. A negative mindset will keep us in the past and hankering for the past, and often, we look at the past with rose-tinted glasses and this prevents us from appreciating the present and definitely keeps us from attaining a great future. A mindset fixed on the past guarantees that you remain stuck.

Progress begins with a progressive mindset. A human mind is constantly working whether we are aware of this or not, and the mind even works when we are not conscious. A progressive mind is always looking ahead and seeks continuous improvement. This mindset always asks, "How can we do this better? Is there no better way of doing things or is this all we got?" The advancements that humanity has made since the beginning of time can be largely attributed to progressive minds. A progressive mind is always consciously at work and it will never rest until results are seen, and once the desired results are attained, this mind begins to explore new avenues and new ways of progressing to another level. "IT IS IMPOSSIBLE FOR A PROGRESSIVE MIND TO GET STUCK."

◆ CONCLUSION

The most striking contrast between stagnation and movement is that stagnation is passive while movement is active, and movement is intentional, while stagnation can be incidental.

A train is of little use if it remains permanently at the station. A grand ship is of no use if it remains permanently docked and never sails and explore the great seas. A sleek sports car that remains stuck in the garage will never provide the thrill that can only be experienced on an open road. A jumbo jet that remains under the hangar will never conquer the skies.

Even a bird that is perched on a branch for too long invites a stone.

It is worth noting that an orchestra performs and produces wonderful melodies in response to the movements of the orchestra conductor; this is the power of movement. Without movement you will never gain ground.

Movement or stagnation can be mental, physical or spiritual. It can happen in the conscious and subconscious faculties. Life is about choices and consequences; make progressive choices always.

CHAPTER TWO

LIFE AND DEATH - MOVEMENT AND STAGNATION

"If you're not moving forward, you're falling back."
- Sam Waterson

◆ A TIME FOR EVERYTHING

One of the Wisdom Books in the Bible is Ecclesiastes and it teaches us the principle of knowing and observing the times. We see this in Ecclesiastes 3:1-4. It says, "There is a time for everything, and a season for every activity under the heavens: a time to be born and a time to die, a time to plant and a time to uproot, a time to kill and a time to heal, a time to tear down and a time to build, a time to weep and a time to laugh, a time to mourn and a time to dance." From this passage of scripture, we can also deduce that there is a time to stay put and a time to move. Animals such as bees, snakes, bats, and bears hibernate during the winter season; this is a requirement for their survival. When the winter period ends, the hibernation must also end and these animals must move out of the hibernation places and resume normal life.

There are times when people live under curfews as the world has experienced such through recent lockdowns due to the Covid-19 pandemic. There have also been curfews or states of emergency in wartimes when people were required to stay indoors or in hiding for their own survival. Even David in the Bible had to spend some time hiding in caves to avoid being killed by Saul, but when the time ended, he emerged and ascended the throne as the king of Israel.

There will be times in our lives when we will need to stay put in a particular place, for example, a place of study, a place of employment, or an association, for a specific time and purpose. Some of the places where we remain for a while are beneficial for our learning, improvement, and growth. For example, someone can be an employee for some time in order to save money and gain skills and insights in order to start their own business.

Someone can decide to remain a student in order to complete post- graduate studies prior to venturing into a career. Another person can continue to stay with their parents until they have saved up enough money for deposit on their own home. The key thing is to ensure that the period of staying put is in line with the plan and purpose of your next move. In the following sections, we see some of the interesting moves and the dangers of not making the necessary moves.

◆ CONCEPTION AND BIRTH THROUGH MOTION

Conception and childbirth are miracles from God, and we see this in various scriptures in the Bible such as 1 Samuel 1:20 where it says, "So it came to pass in the process of time that Hannah conceived and bore a son, and called his name Samuel, saying, 'Because I have asked for him from the Lord." Genesis 18:10 we also see this "And He said, 'I will certainly return to you according to the time of life, and behold, Sarah your wife shall have a son."

The study of Biology teaches us that natural conception and the birth of a child are achieved through motion. The female reproductive system relies on the release of an ovum, which then moves to the fallopian tubes where it can be fertilised when it encounters a sperm. The fertilised ovum must then move through the tube towards the uterus to be implanted on its walls; this is the final step of conception. If any of the movements mentioned fails, then the ovum dies and it is subsequently released from the body and the cycle repeats itself the following month.

The male contributes to the reproductive process by releasing millions of sperms which have to move in semen and be released into the uterus and race against time to stay alive to reach and fertilise the female's ovum. Once the sperm has successfully fertilised the ovum, then the ovum must move from the uterus to the security of the womb. The fetus grows and moves into different positions during the various stages of its development into a baby ready to be born.

As I alluded above, lack of movement by a baby in the womb is a cause for concern for the parents to be; sadly, at times this is a single parent. Irrespective of the parenting circumstances, an immobile baby in the womb has always been a cause of consternation. Equally and by contrast, any movement of the baby in the womb arouses great excitement. We see a great example of this in the following passage of scripture from the Bible in the book of Luke 1:39-41 "Now at this time Mary arose and hurried to the hill country, to a city of Judah (Judea), and she entered the house of Zacharias and greeted Elizabeth. When Elizabeth heard Mary's greeting, her baby leaped in her womb; and Elizabeth was filled with the Holy Spirit and empowered by Him." Elizabeth and Mary had both experienced miraculous, yet different conceptions, with Elizabeth conceiving at a biologically impossible age while

Mary received the immaculate conception through the Holy Spirit.

Although the scriptures do not mention this, it is possible that Elizabeth's baby had stopped moving in the womb hence we see the jubilation when the baby moved upon hearing the greeting from Mary, the soon to be mother of Jesus Christ, the Son of God. Jesus Christ is the source of life and movement and that is why when He appeared – even while still in His mother's womb – there was life-confirming movement in Elizabeth's womb. We see in the scriptures that indeed, He brings life and movement, that is why He says in John 10:10b "but I have come that you may have life and have it more abundantly."

The next big move, the mother of all moves, is the transition of the baby from the mother's womb into the outside world. I call this the mother of all moves as this is the move that kick starts all other movements that we will ever undertake on earth. The movement called "birth" is the physical confirmation of the spiritual phenomenon called "life", once the great move- birth- has been delivered successfully, then all possibilities and impossibilities become probabilities. Life begins through movement.

◆ MOVEMENT OF WATER

The ocean is alive and as a result it is continuously in motion, it casts out anything that is lifeless. The importance of moving water can be seen in John 5:3. It reads: “In these lay a great multitude of sick people, blind, lame, paralyzed, waiting for the moving of the water.” Each time the angel of God moved the water, anyone who went in was healed of whatever disease or infirmity. Rivers have been an important source of life since the beginning of time, and we see this in the introduction where I demonstrated the importance of the life-giving and sustaining power of the Nile.

The movement or flow of water in a river is a catalyst for life and there is no greater demonstration of this than in the Bible in the Book of Ezekiel 47:9 where it says, “And it shall be that every living thing that moves, wherever the rivers go, will live. There will be a very great multitude of fish, because these waters go there; for they will be healed, and everything will live wherever the river goes.”

A flowing river like the one referred to in the above passage of scripture moves life and brings life; it rejuvenates and keeps the waters fresh and life-sustaining. There is nothing that is dead that will remain dead once it comes into contact with this moving river. A river that stops flowing can become a death trap for marine life, so to continue to be alive and give and sustain life, a river must stay in motion. That is why in John 7:38 Jesus Christ likens the Holy Spirit to a life-giving flowing river and He says, “He who believes in me, as the Scripture has said, out of his heart will flow rivers of living water.” The Holy Spirit is moving and flowing like a river and therein lies His life-giving and life-changing power. Keep flowing and you will bring life wherever you go.

◆ THE ECONOMIC FLOW

Economics scholars explain that at the heart of economic activity is movement; goods and services are produced and they are moved to customers and other stakeholders. The movement of goods and services is a catalyst for the movement of money. This becomes a self-fueling cycle of goods, services, and money and it sustains and grows an economy. An interruption and stoppage to this flow or movement can lead to an economic collapse, and this is so even for a booming economy and one that is seemingly invincible. An economy should remain in motion even in the most difficult times because it is more challenging to resuscitate it once it collapses.

There are many economic casualties throughout history when countries fell into a sense of comfort and failed to keep their economies moving and growing. In the book of Matthew 25,

Jesus teaches about the Kingdom of Heaven and uses an economic activity of investing to illustrate. While the main purpose of the parable is to teach about how the Kingdom of God operates, it also confirms how important it is to trade and invest and keep money flowing.

In the parable, a master gave his three servants talents before he travelled to a faraway place for a while. To one servant he gave five talents (money) with which the servant traded or invested and made an additional five talents. Likewise the one who received two talents also traded and made a further two talents. The third servant received one talent, which he buried in the ground.

Upon the master's return, he asked the servant why he kept the talent instead of multiplying it. The servant gave an excuse for not investing or trading with the talent that he had received, and the master was very upset with this servant. The master took a punitive action in Matthew 25:26-28 and it reads; "But his lord answered and said to him, 'You wicked and lazy servant, you knew that I reap where I have not sown, and gather where I have not scattered seed. So you ought to have deposited my money with the bankers, and at my coming I would have received back my own with interest. Therefore take the talent from him, and give it to him who has ten talents." Therefore, God expects you to develop and grow the talent or gift he has deposited in you, by keeping it active. Do not bury it. Remember that if you bury something alive, soon it will die.

◆ ELECTRICITY

The modern economy and way of life are highly dependent on energy, especially electricity. The generation and accessibility of electricity rely on movement; the traditional generation of electricity involves machines that rotate and generate energy which is then transported over electricity networks. The transmission of electricity includes the continuous motion of objects called electrons along a conductive medium.

When the generator stops moving then electricity generation ceases; similarly, when the electrons stop moving the flow of electricity is cut and we experience a loss of electricity supply. There is a small yet fascinating gadget called a "dynamo", it uses the same principles as that of electricity generation through movement. A dynamo is installed on a bicycle and is connected to a lamp that is mounted on the front of the bicycle. At night, when the rider pedals and stays in motion, this produces electricity in the dynamo, which is then used to light the lamp and illuminate the way ahead.

In recent years, South Africa has been experiencing an unpleasant phenomenon called "load shedding". This is essentially a fancy word for planned power cuts, when there are not sufficient generators to provide electricity to meet demand. Load shedding is a result of some of the generators breaking down and therefore not being able to produce electricity. It is apparent from this example that motion brings light, and stagnation brings darkness.

Motion Brings Light, And Stagnation Brings Darkness

◆ A ROLLER-COASTER

A roller-coaster is one of the most loved features of any theme park that is worth its salt. The magic of the roller-coaster is not in its size or design; it is instead in the thrill of the ride when it is in motion. A rollercoaster ride is one of those peculiar and fun activities that both the young and old enjoy and the excitement is generated by the surprise turns and flips. The more varied and unpredictable the movements are, the more exhilarating the experience becomes. The people who lead noteworthy, pioneering, and enviable lives are those who often throw caution to the wind and dare to go on a roller-coaster of life. There are many people who live and die without experiencing the roller-coaster moments of life- being unsure of what would happen next yet remaining excited and expectant. Some movements will look dangerous just like those on a roller-coaster ride; however, without these moves we will not taste the sheer joy of the bliss and beauty of life.

◆ SPORT

A soccer match is fascinating to watch, when you see the players moving and moving the ball around to gain advantage over their opponents. The crescendo of any soccer match is when the ball goes into the net for a goal. Sport in general involves movement of one form or another; the thrill of the 100-metre sprint at a major athletics meeting is always a performance to behold, the sheer speed at which the athletes run is a superbly exhilarating encounter to watch.

A cricketer running to score a winning run is always an occasion to savour. Watching a rugby player outrunning her opponents to score a winning try is a moment worth playing repeatedly. The movement of the body and the head by a boxer to evade the opponent's punches is a skill that is highly prized and it can be the difference between winning and losing a bout.

The graceful movements of a tennis player on the court and the reflexes of hitting the ball to the desired spot and outwitting the opponent is something that never gets stale to watch. The breakneck speed of racing cars whizzing through the circuit is always a spectacle that leaves one short of superlatives that can aptly describe the experience. Even the game of chess, reputed to be a game reserved only for the brainiacs, has its allure in the movements that are made by the protagonists to try to outsmart each other in order to say the famous "check mate" as a confirmation of victory.

Movement is an integral part of sport, and without it, most of the sports would lose their excitement and following and the big paychecks for the sportsmen and women would dry up. We can see that our lives also require movement of one kind or another for there to be joy, excitement, and fulfillment.

◆ THE PULSE AND HEARTBEAT

One of the surest ways to test if a person is alive is to check their pulse. The presence of a pulse confirms that the heart is still pumping blood and that the blood is still circulating through the body, even when a person has lost consciousness. The heartbeat and pulse are both forms of movement. The heartbeat is a throbbing movement that is repetitive and as long as this movement is not halted life can be sustained, while a pulse confirms that the blood that is being pumped by the heart is being moved continually to all organs that require blood for their sustenance. When a heart stops beating or throbbing then a pulse will also stop and death will ensue if there is no timely intervention.

There is a reason why the Bible says in Proverbs 4:23 “Above all else, guard your heart, for everything you do flows from it.” If there is no passion for life in the heart, then there is no meaningful movement that we will undertake, for the source of life is the heart and the source of movement or flow is the very same heart. Feeling stuck? When did you last check the condition of your heart?

◆ A HATCHED EGG

A chicken hen lays eggs and thereafter spends twenty-one days incubating the eggs by continually sitting over them and covering them under its feathers to create the right temperature and conditions for the development of the egg into a chick. At the end of the incubation, the chick must poke the shell from within and force it to crack open, and when that happens the egg is said to have hatched. It is not enough for the egg to hatch; the process is not complete until the chick steps out of the broken shell. That is why when someone who is shy depicts behaviour of being sociable or outgoing they are said to have “come out of their shell”.

It is not good enough for us to remain in the familiar when the time for stepping out of the shell has arrived. Most opportunities are waiting for us to step out and move from the familiar. A chick that breaks the eggshell and yet fails to move out will die even though it would have relished the fresh air of the world outside the shell. If we fail to make the right moves at the appropriate times, some of our dreams and aspirations will die even if all the odds of survival are staked in our favour. A chick that is still in an egg is potential, and potential must not remain potential indefinitely, at some point it needs to be loosened; your potential must not be kept hostage by stagnation. Break the shell, unleash your potential and move into the future filled with awesome experiences and results.

Your Potential Must Not Be Kept Hostage By Stagnation

◆ A SEED TO A TREE

The only time a tree appeared without a seed was at Creation. From that time onwards, God ordained that trees would no longer appear fully grown. The tree begins with a seed which must first move from the storehouse then to the field. At the field, it must move from the hand of a person into the ground. Then it will start growing in the ground until it is ready to move out of the obscurity of the ground and spring forth into the surface where it is then free to grow and flourish.

A seed will never become a tree, unless it keeps moving up. Jesus Christ said unless a seed goes into the ground and dies first, it cannot become a tree, sometimes we are buried and we die, but we must be true seeds that resurrect and rise up to become great trees. Die as a small seed, rise and move from the darkness of the grave. Even if you were buried as the smallest seed, know that you were not buried but planted to rise like a mustard seed, which becomes that great tree that gives life and provides a nesting place for the birds which soar even higher than the tree itself. May your move launch others to greater heights.

◆ THE FOUR LEPROUS MEN

The difference between living and dying can at times be solely dependent on whether we remain stuck or we make a move. There are situations in life that require a decision: to stay or to go? In the book of 2 Kings 7:3, we read the following interesting passage: "Now there were four leprous men at the entrance of the gate; and they said to one another, "Why are we sitting here until we die?"

Leprosy was a deadly, dreaded, and contagious disease in biblical times. This disease affected the skin and in extreme cases, it could disable its victims to a point where they could lose one or more limbs. Biblical scholars explain that due to the contagious nature of the disease as well as its associated stigma, it was a generally accepted practice to banish those afflicted with this disease to isolation and they were often confined to the outskirts of the villages or cities.

In the above scripture, we find what would have been a normal situation of leprous men living outside the city gates; however, this is more remarkable considering that the people in the city - the Israelites - were under siege. The Syrian armies had encamped around the city and no one could come in or go out of the city gates. The standoff and resultant restrictions on movement created a famine situation in the city and death by starvation and malnutrition became an ever-present danger under this condition.

The four leprous men had already been condemned to death through their banishment and we see them contemplating their next move literally and figuratively. These men reached a unanimous decision based on the reality that death was certain if they were to continue being stuck at the gate of the city. Even in their seemingly untenable situation, these men took a critical assessment of their situation and weighed the options that were available to them. However, it is worth noting that the only time they began to explore other options and possibilities was after they realised and concluded that staying stuck was no longer viable. Stagnation presented no possibility of changing the course of what remained of their mortal lives.

We see an interesting discussion by the four lepers about the possible permutations and their subsequent decisive action in verse 4 of the same book of 2 Kings 7 and it says, "If we say, 'We will enter the city,' the famine is in the city, and we shall die there. And if we sit here, we die also. Now therefore, come, let us surrender to the army of the Syrians. If they keep us alive, we shall live; and if they kill us, we shall only die." The Bible records that God had caused fear, panic, and flight of the Syrian armies and they had left their camp in haste, leaving behind money, precious jewels, clothing, and food. By deciding to start moving, the four leprous men stumbled into treasures that they had never imagined.

◆ LAZARUS

We read one of the most remarkable miracles that Jesus Christ performed in the Book of John chapter 11 when He raised a man who had been dead and buried for four days. We read an extract from this section of the Bible and we focus on John 11:41 to 44 and this is what it says, "Then they took away the stone [d] from the place where the dead man was lying. And Jesus lifted up His eyes and said, "Father, I thank You that You have heard Me. And I know that You always hear Me, but because of the people who are standing by I said this, that they may believe that You sent Me." Now when He had said these things, He cried with a loud voice, "Lazarus, come forth!"

And he who had died came out bound hand and foot with grave clothes, and his face was wrapped with a cloth. Jesus said to them, “Loose him, and let him go.”

Jesus Christ raised Lazarus from the dead after He had commanded that the stone that closed the tomb be removed, however all this still required a response from Lazarus. Jesus did not carry Lazarus from the tomb and if Lazarus had chosen to remain in the tomb after being called, he was going to die of starvation or even lack of oxygen had they decided to reclose the tomb on account of him not stepping out. Lazarus responded to the call from Christ and took the steps to move out from what looked like the end and embark on a new beginning. We will also have many calls in our lives where we have to leave a place of death and step forth into new opportunities and endeavours.

Conclusion

Life is measured in movements and lack of movement is akin to death. There are more than enough lessons and demonstrations of these facts. Progress is also measured through moves that we make and stagnation or regress is demonstrated by the moves we fail to make. The life of a human being goes through cycles of movement from which we are to learn. It starts with a movement in the womb, transition from the womb to the outside world, the first tentative and cautious steps of learning to walk. It progresses to moving from the comforts of home into the schooling environment, going to a tertiary institution (when opportunities allow), moving into the world of work or entrepreneurship, moving into marriage and starting a family for those who so elect. Even a hatchling does not stay in its mother's nest, to develop its wings, it needs to step out and take flight and learn to soar to heights previously unknown.

Movement is not only physical, it is also mental, when we decide to explore new ideas and new ways of thinking; sociological, that is when humans move for existential and survival purposes due to environmental changes; political, when people move into new political formations or create new ones in order to re-imagine and pursue greater and better prospects; biological, this includes the transitions that a lava makes in moving from an egg, then a caterpillar, then a pupa, and eventually a beautiful flying butterfly.

If we fail to make the necessary moves, then we fail to live even when God has given us the gift of life. We will not be able to enjoy life and discover all its limitless possibilities until we make the required moves at the required intervals of our lives. It is not by mistake that life is called a journey; it is called thus because true living is demonstrated in motion.

True Living Is Demonstrated In Motion

CHAPTER THREE

LIFE AND DEATH IN MANY SHAPES AND SIZES

"What good is living a life you've been given if all you do is stand in one place." - Anonymous

---

Small, there are things oval and things rectangular, there are things wide and things thin, there are things high and things low. Death also comes similarly, in shapes and sizes; we have witnessed great empires dying and we have equally witnessed insignificant empires dying. Every living organism including humans will die at some point as nothing is meant to live eternally here on earth. The Bible confirms this in Ecclesiastes 9:5a and it says, "For the living know that they will die." However, it is better to be alive than dead if we can help it and the same book of Ecclesiastes 9:4 captures this perfectly and it says, "But for him who is joined to all the living there is hope, for a living dog is better than a dead lion."

There are numerous examples in life of people and organisations that got stuck and died. Life and death come in many shapes, sizes, and ways as we discover below.

◆ JOBS HERE, JOBS GONE

There are jobs that look solid and stable currently, but history is replete with many jobs that were seemingly secure but before people knew it, those jobs were gone. Over the past 100 years some of the following jobs and or industries have disappeared or have been reduced drastically from the world of work:

Farm work – there are some manual and labour intensive jobs that used to be performed in the agricultural sector in the early 1900s to the 1960s. At the turn of the last century, the majority of people in the world worked on both small and large-scale farms. However, with the increasing mechanisation and automation, many of these jobs have become obsolete and efficient machines have replaced labourers.

Work in the Horse Transportation Industry – in the era when horses were the main mode of transport, there were jobs and industries that were thriving in support of this form of mobility. These industries created jobs such as manufacturing of wheels, carriages, horseshoes, saddles, and whips. It is remarkable that there were also people employed to clean the excrement of horses from the streets as you can imagine what peak traffic used to leave behind on busy days. All these jobs have either disappeared or the few that remain, such as manufacturing of horse equipment such as saddles and horseshoes, have become very miniscule and also depend on mechanisation.

Work in the Railway Industry – this industry was revolutionised by the invention of the steam engine and for many decades since the turn of the last century, the railway became the key transportation system to drive industry, industrialisation, and economies of many countries. The proliferation of cars, light delivery vehicles and long-haul trucks have reduced the reliance on rail transport in many countries and the rail industry accounts for far less volumes of goods that are moved around. The past two decades have also seen reduction in air freight costs and this has also added more pressure to the rail industry. All these changes in the freight industry have led to a great reduction in railway job opportunities and careers in these industries. One study indicated that in the USA the rail industry employed 3% of the workforce some 70 years ago and this has dropped to 0,1% in recent years; this is quite a major drop in the numbers.

Typist – this used to be a highly sought after and rare skill. The typewriter had its era when there was very little room allowed for error. At the time this type of work was one of the most popular careers especially in corporate. However, with the advent of personal computers, laptops, smartphones and tablets, virtually everyone is able to type their own documents and a typist is no longer required nor viable. The few people who perform the typing function in organisations are actually doing it as part of general administrative work, but it is no longer a stand-alone and dedicated function or job.

Film projectionist – the advent of cinema and the use of projectors and film led to the creation of this job to serve in this booming industry within entertainment. The modern cinema is digital and it no longer requires a projectionist as films are loaded and played electronically, and these can even be pre-programmed for the day or even for a week with minimal human intervention thereafter. This role of the film projectionist has now been dealt a deathblow with no prospects of a resurrection any time soon.

Bowling Ball Pinsetter – The game of pinball bowling is one of the oldest games since the advent of gaming arcades; it is reputed to have started in the 1930s in America. It is a fun activity that the whole family can enjoy, young and old, male and female. The game of pinball bowling involves rolling a ball on a specially made “roll-way” towards ten pre-arranged pins, and the plan is to knock the pins with the ball at one go. There was a job called a Bowling Ball Pinsetter, this person would always arrange the pins after each round of play. With the advent of technology, the machine arranges and resets the pins and this job has become extinct. Imagine if this was all you did or knew? Scary!

Work in Factory Assembly Lines – the second industrial revolution included the boom in manufacturing and factories with massive assembly lines became the norm and the standard for large-scale production. The assembly line was one of the early innovations to improve efficiencies, streamline work, and improve productivity. These early assembly line arrangements were very labour intensive in that every part of the production line required one or more human beings to man. The modern assembly line is almost entirely automated, and a similar production factory that would employ, for example, 1000 people in the 1950s can operate and produce the same output with a workforce of 50 to 100 workers. Most of the manual jobs in factories have become obsolete. Those workers that never reskilled are probably now jobless.

Those Workers That Never Reskilled Are Probably Now Jobless

JOBS EXTINCTION IS CALLING

They say history is the best teacher, from the history of the jobs and careers that disappeared or have experienced a catastrophic decline as seen above, we can learn that this pattern will surely repeat itself in future, it is just a question of when. Numerous jobs are very strong contenders for extinction in the next 10 to 20 years, due mainly to the rapid increase of 4IR technologies such as robotics and other forms of artificial intelligence. A few of these jobs are worth looking at as I have done below:

Bank Tellers – The banking industry has been at the cutting edge of technological advancements. The cardless banking transactions that include cash deposits at ATMs have led to reduced numbers of bank tellers in many banks across the world. Numerous banks do not allow cash deposits or cash withdrawals below a certain amount.

In addition, the use of cashless purchases and payments is set to further reduce the need for transactions involving cash, especially within the bank. All these changes and further developments will make bank tellers eventually redundant; there will be no role for them, or the numbers can reduce to just one teller per bank branch for special and adhoc cash transactions. The likelihood is that the bank teller function will be part of multiple roles that the “teller” of the future would be responsible for. For the rest of the tellers, keep moving!

Telemarketers/Call Centre Agents – few of us relish a call from a telemarketer, because often times we are not looking for what they are trying to sign us up for; and if we need services or products that they market, we ordinarily know where to look. Calling a call centre and waiting for what feels like an eternity to hear a human voice on the other side can be an unpleasant experience that we avoid where possible. The sales pitch of a telemarketer is mostly scripted and it is for this reason that some organisations have started to use scripted automated messages to market products.

Similarly, some call centres have been automated and help is available without a need to speak to a human agent on the other side. The continuous adoption of technology as the norm will render the telemarketer and call centre agent jobs obsolete sooner than most of these employees realise.

Insurance Industry Workers – the insurance industry has been around for way more than a century. The work in this industry, like many other industries, has been the preserve of human beings. However, with the advancements in technology and automation, machines will perform some of the work such as recording data and quantifying claims leading to a great reduction in employment opportunities in this line of work.

Paralegal – these are jobs that support lawyers and require a certain aptitude on legal matters. One of the core functions of this role is to gather and study precedence in law and outcomes of similar cases in order to prepare for new cases. However, with the filing and record keeping from the legal industry over the years, this function can easily be programmed into an intelligent machine that can search, collect and analyse historical legal cases and formulate some of the key defence arguments. It is evident that this function is at risk of being taken over by machines, or the numbers of such practitioners will reduce greatly in the future.

Factory Workers – one can sympathise greatly with factory workers, as this type of work has already suffered great losses in terms of employment since the introduction of the automated assembly line. The job bloodbath is set to continue into the future as the artificial intelligence gains even more ground and momentum due to the ongoing developments. The number of factory workers will reduce to negligible levels in the coming five to ten years and this industry may be the hardest hit of all industries that are faced with major drops in job numbers.

Bricklayers – this is one of the oldest professions since man began to construct buildings with brick and mortar. The increase in the need for quality workmanship and attention to detail, cost, and speed of construction led to bricklaying becoming a specialised and highly sought after skill. This continued and gained even more prominence with the advent of skyscrapers and other bespoke buildings that required due care and skill of a specialist bricklayer. It would have been unthinkable a few years ago that this skill will become less important, especially considering that construction has been one of the hallmarks of the modern economy for centuries.

However, due to the advancements in construction technology and artificial intelligence, specialised machines are now able to do bricklaying with greater quality, speed, and precision. Their quality of work surpasses that of the best bricklayer in the world. The number of bricklaying jobs are set to dwindle in the coming years, especially in the developed economies.

Accountants – accounting and economic activity have been joined at the proverbial hip for as long as mankind began to trade. In its early form the accounting function was performed manually- with pen and paper calculations and records. The advancements in calculators and computer technology ushered a new era of technology-based systems, programs and processes to perform accounting functions, including data transfer and record-keeping.

Technological advancements continue to scale new and previously unimaginable heights and this is reducing the reliance on human accountants for most of the accounting functions. If anyone had even dared to suggest twenty years ago that this skill would become less important, such a person's mental faculties would have been called into question, considering that for millennia the accounting profession has been one of the most prestigious and elite professions in the world economy. There is an increasing prospect of unemployment or reduced employment for accountants as machines continue to take over.

COMPANIES AND PRODUCTS THAT DIED IN STAGNATION

There are upswings and downturns, things come and go as the saying goes, and this applies to organisations, products, and services as it does with us humans. History is replete with organisations both large and small rising and falling, living and dying, as well as products and services that were once abuzz with life but have since died or had near- death experiences. Stagnation is one of the most commonly cited death knells of organisations, especially companies throughout the world for as long as industry and commerce have been in existence.

The field of marketing strategy introduces us to a concept called "first mover advantage". A first mover is a company that makes a decision to pioneer or chart a new course by introducing a new product or service, or enhances an existing product or service. There are companies that use a follower strategy, by observing the first movers and then learning from them and entering the market with a competitor service or product, with better features or some offerings.

The last category of companies are those that make no move, but rely on the hope that their products or service offerings are already superior and face no threats from actions of the first mover and followers. As with everything, there are advantages and disadvantages for being a first mover, for being a follower and for making no move at all. However, the notion that one's current products and/or service offering are robust enough to withstand changes made by competitors can be a very dangerous approach to business; as a result, the no-move approach has led to many corporate casualties, and this is set to continue for as long as businesses exist. The business environment is so fluid and fast- paced that some of the changes are not even triggered by competitors in your sector but by external factors and shifts and this may require a response from any company that wants to remain in business.

Some companies, businesses, products, and services have died and others failed to maintain their stature mainly due to failure to read and move with the tide. The examples discussed below provide irrefutable evidence of the killer called stagnation:

Kodak – this company dominated the photographic film industry for the longest time, and it had no real competition. But the advent of digital photography and the failure by Kodak to make a responsive move to this technological shift dealt a death blow to the company's dominance and profitability. It is reputed that a Kodak engineer actually came up with the initial design for a digital camera, but the company's management dismissed the idea as a fancy invention with no real potential, as a result, they failed to benefit from what could have provided a first mover advantage and a sizeable market share to go with it. The failure to make neither a proactive nor responsive move cost Kodak dearly as the company filed for bankruptcy in 2012.

Movie Rental Shops – the video shop as it was commonly known was a standard feature in virtually every town and city. This business, to the uninitiated, was essentially a library of VHS tapes, and later DVDs, that could be rented for an average period of one to three days. These shops had all categories of movies, some series and documentaries. In many urban households, family time on weekends revolved around renting a movie (or a few) and preparing homemade popcorns and enjoying watching the movies in the comfort of their homes. The advancements and accessibility of pay TV and in recent years the growth of streaming entertainment services has almost eradicated the video shop as we know it. The people who owned these business had gold in terms of customer base and information, and they could have used these to relaunch into another industry or played in the streaming game. Today they are possibly out of business and their workers are unemployed as their industry evolved but they were unable to make a move.

Nokia – for the longest time in the 1990s Nokia and cellphone were synonymous, that is how iconic the brand was in the telecommunications industry. The company was always at the cutting edge of technology and it occupied the position of market leader in virtually every country where cellphones were in use. The technological sands were unfortunately shifting right underneath Nokia's feet and the company was overtaken by what used to be virtually unknown brands such as Samsung and Blackberry, and in recent years the iPhone and Huawei. Nokia is still in the cellphone business but they are a shadow of their former selves in this market, due to inability to make the right and timely moves.

BlackBerry – this cellphone brand was built around exclusivity, and this is a profitable approach to business if it can be sustained, where a company focuses on a niche market with specialised and customised products and services. The BlackBerry security features and information encryption were unmatched in its industry. Perhaps one of the biggest selling points for Blackberry was its exclusive and closed messaging platform called Blackberry Messanger (BBM). This allowed mostly BlackBerry users to make voice calls and message each other using this closed platform. Sadly, it was this very unique feature of BBM that put paid to Blackberry's popularity and prestige with the introduction of free and inexpensive messaging solutions such as multimedia messaging service (MMS), WhatsApp, and other open-access messaging solutions. Blackberry failed to read the tide and what was a pioneering company has been reduced to a sideshow in the highly competitive cellphone industry; if only they had got their move on.

Commodore Corp – many people would probably ask: "Commodore what?" As most people associate the Commodore name with a legendary American RnB and Soul group with hit songs from the 1970s all the way to the early 1990s, which eventually launched the solo career of one Lionel Richie. Commodore Corp was a personal computer manufacturing company in the 1970s and 1980s, however this company failed to stay in motion in the highly competitive and innovative computer industry. The company eventually filed for bankruptcy in 1994. In an environment and industry where movement is life, the company died primarily because it failed to keep its move on.

Sony Walkman – in the 1980s and early 1990s owning a Sony Walkman was akin to owning the latest and most advanced cellphone in the current times. The Walkman was a very portable mini-cassette player that had earphones and one could carry it and listen to music (or any recording) while walking and travelling on any mode of transport, hence the name “Walkman”. Like many other companies in history, Sony rested on its Walkman laurels and failed to read the game with the advent of technologically advanced music-playing products like the i-Pod and recently the use of smartphones and other gadgets which include streaming and buying of music and other content online. How Sony failed to lead in the digital transformation is a testimony of the suicidal nature of stagnation.

Hummer – one of the most iconic cars in movies and music videos of the late 1990s to the early 2000s. The yellow Hummer used to feature prominently in many dreams of the young and upwardly mobile of that era. The rise in oil and fuel prices in the 2000s, as well as the increasing focus on reduction in carbon emissions and the drive towards greater efficiency made the gas-guzzlers like the Hummer become less popular. The combination of innovations and technology in compact and affordable cars, introduction of a variety of competitively priced SUVs, especially from South Korea, China, and India, as well as the economic difficulties in many countries led to dwindling demand for cars like the Hummer. The Hummer failed to move swiftly and nimbly into the future and the company closed shop in 2009.

◆ ECONOMIC LIFE AND DEATH

History shows us some interesting economic and power shifts from the earliest years of human endeavour. Economics as a field of study primarily focuses on the production, distribution, and consumption of goods and services within a country, region, or the world with some form of payment or transactions relating to this movement of these goods and services. It is clear that movement, and the correct movement of goods and services with the corresponding and commensurate move of money is at the heart of economic performance and growth.

Economic Performance Is About Movement Or Lack Thereof

The growth or decline of economies depends highly on how well or poorly they manage these movements. There are other factors such as price movements, supply and demand, availability of resources and other economic factors, but ultimately economic performance is about movement or lack thereof. We can look at a few economies that died or lived and can see the common mistakes of some in contrast with the astuteness of others:

Syria – war is one of the surest ways to collapse an economy, Syria is one of the countries that have sadly been in the grip of an unceasing war in recent years. One of the problems with war is that it stops or limits the free movement of goods and services as well as the movement of money. The economic difficulties in Syria demonstrate the dangers of lack of movement with regards to economic activity.

Afghanistan – this country has also been reeling from one level of war to another. Endless wars, continued instability, and low investments have collectively conspired against this economy. The World Bank identifies one of the major inhibitors of the Afghan economy as the inability to find and leverage sources of sustainable growth, and we know that growth is positive movement. Another hindrance to the economy of this country is the lack of infrastructure to move goods and services to the markets, be it domestically, regionally and internationally; this highlights once more the importance of movement in any economy.

Venezuela – this country was booming during the period of high oil prices and high demand for oil in the world. The country failed to read the economic tide and was unable to flow and stay on course when oil prices dropped and demand for oil fell. The country failed to move timeously in diversifying its economy, and unfortunately the citizens are feeling more than a pinch and this has seen many emigrating for them to survive and this further makes the economic recovery a mammoth task.

Zimbabwe – since its independence in 1980, the Zimbabwean economy was stable and growing to a point where the country was considered a breadbasket of Africa and southern Africa in particular. Because of the economic performance, the country was able to invest in education and it produced some of the best engineers, medical professionals, academics, corporate leaders, and tradesmen. However, the political turmoil and mismanagement of the country's economy hampered the production and movement of goods and services especially in the agriculture and mining sectors, which formed the backbone of the economy, and sadly the situation has not been remedied to this day. The country failed to leverage from the gains it had made and did not move into higher levels of economic development and the tragedy continues to unfold.

South Korea – this country has recorded remarkable economic growth over the past half century. The country started as an agriculture-dependent economy with little prospects of industrialisation. The policy makers in the country realised the importance of the movement of goods, especially to export markets, and this led to the creation of an economic environment that supported innovation and an investment friendly economic system. As a result, the country is a key player in electronic goods, automobile industry, petrochemicals, and ship manufacturing, all of which require continuous innovation. Today the country is in the top ten exporters in the world. Talk about leveraging and benefiting from movement to drive economic growth and performance.

China – this is another country in the Far East, which was historically operating as an agrarian economy, with low literacy and skills level. The country made a bold decision to open some areas of its economy and to restructure into a technology and innovation driven economy. There was a deliberate and coordinated investment in education and training, and through these China was able to lift more than 500 million people out of abject poverty. In a period of a quarter of a century, the country moved from back waters to occupy the position of the second biggest economy in the world. When one looks at the picture of a small fishing town in

1993 and the modern-day metropolis called Shanghai with its cutting- edge technology and infrastructure, the results are astounding, and as they say, a picture speaks a thousand words. China decided to move and stay in motion, and the results are there for all to see.

United Arab Emirates – this country is in the middle of the desert in the Middle East. It was an impoverished country until the discovery of oil and the ensuing industrialisation, which was driven by investments in human capital. The country used the oil revenues to build modern infrastructure, educate its citizenry, and grow its economy beyond historically unprecedented levels, and today it has one of the highest standards of living in the world. The analysis of the oil reserves has revealed that the country will run out of oil over the next half century.

This could have been a death knell for the country, however the forward looking and innovation leaders of the UAE thought of the next move, then put that next move into motion by positioning their country as the next trade and tourism hub of the world. The country is already investing and constructing tourism infrastructure, which includes airports, hotels, conference facilities, as well as man-made islands. To highlight the importance of movement, the Dubai airport is a popular transit point for connecting flights for travel across the world.

◆ CHURCH IN MOTION

The Church of Christ was commissioned by Jesus Christ to be evangelical, that means to continually move and spread the Gospel of the Lord. The Apostle Paul, with some help from his select co-servants, such as Mark, Timothy, Barnabas, and Silas, established and grew the early church on this principle and approach. The results of their work can be seen through some of the churches that they planted and which helped to keep the Gospel moving, some of these churches are introduced below:

- Thessalonica – this was in the region then known as Macedonia in northern Greece. This was a port city situated on a major trade route.
- Corinth – this was a port city which was a major destination for a variety of travellers for business and leisure, and it was in the eastern Mediterranean region of Achaia, which is in present day Greece. It was a cosmopolitan city and also a major trade route of the time.
- Philippi - this city was another thriving urban centre in the east of Macedonia. There were gold mines near the

city and as a result, different classes and nationalities were drawn to this place.

- Colossae was a city in the Roman province of Asia Minor, in what is modern day Turkey. This City was a major trade hub, and was also renowned for special cloth manufacturing.
- Galatia – ancient Galatia was also in present-day Turkey and it was a Roman province, which was near the seas and it had a multi-layered and mixed society although it was not a major trade centre.
- Ephesus – This city was in present day Turkey and it was a port city which was once one of the major trade centres in the Mediterranean region. It was a cosmopolitan society with a multifaceted community.
- Laodicea – this was one of the largest metropolis of the ancient world. Due to its size, location, and economy this area was one of the major trade centres and it was also a key trade route connecting various cities and regions during that time. It was located in present day Turkey.

The locations of these churches show a common thread of mostly bustling cities, major trade routes, cosmopolitan societies, with continuous movement. This was a perfect way to keep the message moving and spreading quickly. The identification of these strategic locations was in line with Jesus Christ's great commission in Matthew 28:19, which says, "Go therefore and make disciples of all the nations, baptizing them in the name of the Father and of the Son and of the Holy Spirit."

In our modern era, we have witnessed the work of great evangelists. Two of the foremost evangelists of our era, who were responsible for bringing millions of souls to Christ, are Billy Graham and Reinhard Bonnke. These men understood more than many that the church has to keep moving, no wonder the Bible says in Isaiah 52:7a, "How beautiful and delightful on the mountains are the feet of him who brings good news." To continually bring the good news, the feet need to keep moving. A church that fails to evangelise and get the message of the Gospel to new recipients will eventually die because it is failing on two key principles, namely, disobedience to the Word of God and failure to recognise that stagnation leads to death. If one were to make an observation of churches that have died, stagnation will list high among the reasons for death. Church, Go Ye! Lives and souls depend on this!

To continually bring the good news, the feet need to keep moving

---

Many companies, product lines, and service offerings that are on a path to extinction, some are on expensive life support to avoid the inevitable. When last did you take stock of your career, your business, your product, your service, your niche, and what are the prospects of survival, let alone success, looking like in the next five to years? It is time for a reality check, and to get your move on!

CHAPTER FOUR

MOVE STOPPERS

"Don't let yesterday take up too much of today." - Anonymous

Human beings are instinctively wired to resist change. Movement in its true essence is a form of change, because it is supposed to start at one place and end at a different place, be it physical, psychological, economical, biological, political or spiritual, and everything else in between. People, organisms, countries, systems and institutions that move are those that are not resistant to change.

For many of us change is more often than not a very daunting thought, and as a result, we will always work extremely hard to find what would pass as valid and convincing reasons why movement is not an option. There are numerous reasons that have been given by each of us at different stages of our lives, explaining why it is impossible to move; there have also been underlying reasons in the subconscious mind that have forced many into a state of permanent and normalised stagnation. A few of the sources of reluctance to move are worth exploring.

◆ PAST FAILURES AND SUCCESSES

Any person who has lived beyond teenage years has recorded some victories and memorable successes to be proud of; on the flip side of the coin there are loses and failures of various magnitude and impact. The failures and successes, losses and victories are equally dangerous as they can equally encourage and justify stagnation. There is a problem of being stuck in a continuous state of celebration, or basking in past glory as the saying goes. There is also the very present danger of having suffered too many bruising losses that settling in the losing corner of stagnation becomes normal and is nothing to be overly concerned about. If you do not view and handle past success and failure correctly, they have the potential to keep you locked in stagnation that is fed and sustained by history.

To move there needs to be a constant review and analyses of the past successes and failures in their correct context. The past victories must serve as motivation that more can still be achieved if we keep moving ahead, the good old days must be the fuel that we need to take the next step by reminding ourselves that more is possible as long as we keep progressing. Past failures must be used as lessons to see what changes are needed if we are to turn these disappointments into great celebrations in future, we need to move past the pain and regret of failure and loss, and dust ourselves off and believe that there is more that life can still deliver if we stay in motion. Haggai 2:9a reminds us that "The glory of this latter house shall be greater than of the former....", and this must be our attitude towards life, that no matter what happened in the past, greater glory lies ahead and it cannot be apprehended while we are stuck in the past.

Greater Glory Lies Ahead And It Cannot Be Apprehended While We Are Stuck In The Past

---

◆ PRESENT CIRCUMSTANCES

There is great influential power in a person's current circumstances. The circumstances can block the view of the future, especially if the circumstances appear to be an insurmountable mountain with no prospects of ever being scaled. Sadly, some of the mountains in our present circumstances are in fact mole hills which our imagination has magnified into colossal mountain ranges. Current circumstances can create a comfort zone and a false sense of security, and can be a great hindrance to progress. Unfortunately, for as long as we are alive we will always have to face and deal with current circumstances.

In order to move we have to be able to momentarily step out of our current circumstances. This would allow us to have the correct perspective on the current reality within the context of the big picture which goes beyond the immediate realities of life. The inability to break free from the realities of today has caused many people to remain stuck in their circumstances, because we are not able to think of moving from what appears to be a place of permanent residence. There are people who are stuck in current situations that are not serving their best interests, and neither are these aligned with the desired future destination. Many people settled in the comfort of their current circumstances that they did not perceive that the sand was shifting right under their comfortable feet until it was too late.

Once you have recognised and acknowledged that the prevailing circumstances are not beneficial nor useful for your progress, you have to get your move on. One great example of a realisation of circumstances that need to change is found in the situation of the so-called prodigal son in the book of Luke 15. After this son asks for his portion of the inheritance from his father he goes to a distant country where he squanders all the wealth on prodigal living. He then hits hard times and ends up being employed to feed pigs, and eating with them. In Luke 15:17 the Bible says, "He came to himself" and when he conceded that the circumstances were untenable and no longer useful, he decided to change and move back home. It is not enough for us to come to ourselves or back to our senses; the realisation that our current circumstances are not serving us must lead to us making a move to change the situation. Do not be stuck in circumstances, decide and get your move on!

◆ THE COMPANY WE KEEP

There is a well-known saying that goes: "birds of a feather flock together", this simply says people keep company and associate with those with similar interests and inclinations. If you are not of a particular feather and hang around that feather, eventually you will assimilate into it. There are people who did not drink and ended up drinking just by hanging around those who drink; people who did not like fashion ended up liking it by hanging with "fashionistas"; sadly, some people who were not criminals became criminals just by spending inordinate amount of time with criminals.

At various stages of our lives we find ourselves in associations or friendships that appear to be mostly incidental and not deliberately planned and pursued. There are gravitational forces that pull one towards like-minded people; however, the next move in your life may require a different mindset that is not currently a feature in your immediate circle. Tragically, there are some associations that one can get into that actually sabotage the future or do not allow one to make the move that one needs to make to go to the next level or assignment of life. That is why it is important to take stock and evaluate your network to see if it adds value, helps one to progress, and is aligned with one's future aspirations.

As we grow there has to be a deliberate and intentional choice regarding the associations, partnerships, and friendships that we become part of. Scientists, politicians, philosopher, pastors, scholars, believers, entrepreneurs, all have their own circles with like-minded people.

The Bible warns about the wrong company in 1 Corinthians 15:33 and it says, "Do not be misled: 'Bad company corrupts good character." This is also reiterated by Psalm 1:1 where it says, "Blessed is the man who walks not in the counsel of the ungodly, nor stands in the path of sinners, nor sits in the seat of the scornful." To further see the importance of the circles we belong to we can also check Proverbs 13:20 where it provides this piece of wisdom, "He who walks [as a companion] with wise men will be wise, but the companions of [conceited, dull-witted] fools [are fools themselves and] will experience harm."

Another category of people that can cause stagnation are the "dream killers". These are people who drain you by their incessant negativity and pessimism, the ones who encourage you to maintain the status quo of stagnation. The perennial pessimist discourages you from attempting anything without even taking the trouble to convince you as to why the current circumstances are more viable, neither will they provide you with another option whatsoever. Imagine in the midst of a famine, if Isaac had said to pessimists, "I am going to plant, and I am expecting a great harvest", they would have told him how reckless and wasteful he was to throw seed to a ground that was currently yielding nothing. Fortunately, he did not seek the approval of naysayers, but he made a move and planted and in seemingly hopeless conditions, he harvested a hundred fold, yes a hundred fold!

If you want to move to new things, it is self-sabotage to hang around people who prefer the status quo and they have all manner of reasons and justifications why remaining stuck is a viable option. Proverbs 27:17 teaches that "Iron sharpens iron, and one man sharpens another." If you desire something different, identify those who reflect or represent it and begin to move towards their circle, if this fails, create your own circle.

Remember a circle is not wrong in itself; it is only wrong when it does not serve your purpose or propel you to your desired destiny. You will not be a sharpened iron if you keep hanging around rotten apples. David did not hang around with the soldiers whom Goliath intimidated. Joseph could not remain long with his brothers because he was a dreamer and they were not. Sometimes the first move you have to make is to get out of the wrong circle.

You Will Not Be A Sharpened Iron If You Keep Hanging Around Rotten Apples

---

◆ LACK OF OPPORTUNITIES AND RESOURCES

Life on earth requires opportunities and resources. Almost everything we pursue will ultimately involve leveraging from opportunities and resources that come to our disposal. It is therefore natural and normal that before we think of making any move we would consider the availability of opportunities and resources to facilitate that intended move. Ecclesiastes

9:11 teaches us a profound lesson about life and resources, and it says, "Again I saw that under the sun the race is not to the swift, nor the battle to the strong, nor bread to the wise, nor riches to the intelligent, nor favor to those with knowledge, but time and chance happen to them all." This scripture tells us that all of us have been given opportunities and resources and the magnitude or multitude of these should not hinder our pursuit of our goals. When opportunities arise we must seize them and make our move, similarly we are to use the resources at our disposal.

We have all looked at making a potentially good move, yet got ourselves discouraged because we did not have the required resources or the opportunity was not extended to us. It is lamentable that some of the opportunities and resources that we claim to lack are in fact a figment of our imaginations, and as such they are merely perceived and not real. It is therefore not surprising that often times God has used what appeared to be very little or insignificant to demonstrate to us that what we have and consider inadequate may be just what is needed for that next step.

When God called Moses to free the children of Israel from bondage and slavery, He asked Moses what he had in his hand, and Moses only had a rod, but God turned this rod into a snake and used the same rod to perform miracles and eventually delivered freedom for the Israelites. In the book of Judges we also read about a man called Gideon whom the angel of God saluted as a "mighty man of valour" a seemingly very strange accolade considering that this man was in fear and threshing wheat to go hide it from the Midianites who were terrorising Israel at the time. When God sent Gideon to deliver victory for the Israelites, He said to Gideon: "...Go in this might of yours..." Although Gideon was powerless, God saw a man of valour hidden in the fearful individual.

For the longest time Joseph appeared to have only dreams and a colourful coat, and his brothers mocked him for this. But it was the very dreams that moved him from being sold as a slave, ending up in prison wrongfully, and eventually occupying the prime minister's position in a foreign country of Egypt. I can imagine that there were many Egyptians who were better qualified, had better resources, who had the right connections, who were born into royalty, who felt that they deserved the prime minister's position better than Joseph, yet all it took was the dream and the ability to interpret dreams.

In the book of Judges, we also read of another man called Samson who used a fresh jawbone of a donkey to kill 1000 men. A dead donkey is considered one of the most useless things in the world, yet its jawbone became a great weapon in the hands of Samson. In the book of 2 Kings chapter 4 we read about a widow who cried unto the Prophet Elisha as her deceased husband owed people money, and they wanted to take her sons as a form of payment. Elisha asked the woman a seemingly useless and irrelevant question, given the circumstances and her tearful plea; he said to her, "what do you have in the house?" The widow answered that she had nothing except a little oil, which she considered to be nothing because of its quantity. The prophet instructed her to borrow vessels and pour the oil into those, she filled many vessels and there was enough oil to pay the debt, and enough money left over for her and her family to live off.

We have read how many of the great tech companies of Silicon Valley were started in the basement or garages with very little except the will to take a step towards creating something new. Sometimes we fail to see what we already have and as a result, we remain in the death of stagnation. We need to start with what we have and take the first step in the very place where there appears to be very little, what appears little has potential to catapult you into the next level.

What Appears Little Has Potential To Catapult You Into The Next Level

---

◆ MINDSET

There is a quote by Oliver Wendell Homes, Jr that I like which talks about the movement of the mind through stretching it. It says: "A mind that is stretched by a new experience can never go back to its old dimensions." The mind was designed to stay progressive; a mind that stays idle for too long dies to new ideas. The mind is also the battlefield or the place of continuous contestation, and exploration of what option to take when one faces a dilemma. All these demonstrate the importance of the mind in the life of a person, and this perhaps explains the difficult and tragic decisions that loved ones have to make when a person is diagnosed to be medically brain dead.

The mind is also a fertile soil, and it will always grow whatever is planted in it, unless this is uprooted before it takes root. Psychologists have explained the importance of paying attention to our thoughts. They advise that what we think about often and how we think about it influences the habits that we eventually develop. This highlights the importance of paying attention to our thought patterns and the mindsets we develop. 2 Corinthians 10:5b emphasises the importance of consciously thinking about the thoughts that we allow to take root in our minds, it says "… and we take captive every thought to make it obedient to Christ." It is important to pay attention to our thoughts, our thought patterns and the mindsets which we develop and rely on to navigate through life. A mindset is a general outlook, view, and approach to life. We can see that our mindsets will either hinder us from moving or they will help us to be open and accommodative to moving and change.

We must avoid a rigid mindset as this type of mindset will always oppose any plans of making a move in any area of our lives. A wrong mindset is prone to bouts of doubt, self-pity, indecision, excuses, risk aversion and all these are a sure path to stagnation. A murmuring and complaint-prone mindset is bound to cause us to get stuck and die in the wilderness and fail to reach the promised land which God has allocated to each of us in our lifetimes.

We need to develop mindsets that enable change, growth, and all-round progress, instead of settling for the mundane and moribund life that we see all around us. The mind must be intentionally and continually engaged, exercised, stretched through exposure to positive and constructive stimuli; so set your mind on the right mindset. If we do not arrest our thoughts, they will arrest and imprison us in stagnation.

◆ HEART CONDITION

The Bible teaches us in the book of Proverbs 4:23 where it says, "Above all else, guard your heart, for everything you do flows from it." This scripture reveals the importance of the condition of our hearts because all endeavours are conceived in the heart. A heart condition is not a disease but rather the condition or state of our hearts. The condition of the heart will determine whether we are inclined to make any move or certain moves. What fills our hearts will determine what drives us, and even the lack of drive in worst case scenarios.

The contents of our hearts will always influence our minds and our thinking patterns and the habits that we create and live by. Our dreams, desires and aspirations are hatched in the depths of our hearts and they manifest themselves as thoughts and ideas that we then crystalise and decide whether to pursue or not. If something has taken root in our hearts, it becomes very difficult for our minds to just dismiss it.

The heart is the dwelling place of our emotions. We hate through the heart; we despise through the heart; we adore through the heart; and we love through the heart. We even believe through the heart as the Bible also teaches us. We need to continually check the condition of our hearts because its contents will most likely determine whether we will decide to make the necessary moves in life. It is not possible to make meaningful moves and to stay the course of the move if our hearts are not in the move. If the heart is not pumped up for the move, then that move is doomed. When it comes to making a move and staying the course, a strong heart is better than a strong mind with a weak heart. Visit and purify your heart often; it will definitely take you into the next phase of your life.

There Are Few Things In Life That Cause Stagnation More Than Fear

---

◆ FEAR

There are few things in life that cause stagnation more than fear. Fear has many synonyms such as fright, panic, distress, consternation, dread, anxiety, all of which are words that exude negativity. Fear paralyses an able-bodied person; it makes them fail to exercise mobility. It is clear that fear can make us see the prospects of failure while obstructing our view of the endless possibilities. William Shakespeare said that "a coward dies a thousand times before his death." This shows the negative power of fear in that it can create a danger from nothing and it can magnify minor huddles into endless pits of destruction. In making a move there are many fears that may encroach on us like a thief in the night, such as fear of failure, fear of feeling inadequate or ill-equipped, fear of ridicule, fear of retribution, fear of lack of support, fear of opposition, even fear of the unknown. It is not by accident, but rather by design, that the Bible is reputed to mention the phrase "Fear Not" or

"Do not be afraid" 365 times, one preacher says this means there is a "Fear Not" each day of each year of our lives.

If we allow fear to rule us, we will continue to discourage ourselves from making moves that usher us to a brighter and greater future; that is why the Bible tells us that fear causes torment. If David had been afraid like the army of Israel, he would not have slayed the giant and become the respected and celebrated king that we speak about. In the book of Matthew chapter 14, we see one of the most remarkable miracles where Jesus walked on water towards the boat in which His disciples were riding. Peter, one of disciples, asked Jesus to bid him to come on the water, and in verse 29 Jesus called Peter onto the water and he stepped out of the water and began to walk on it. But as soon as Peter focused on the wind and became afraid, he began to sink and Jesus caught and saved him.

If we allow fear to overpower us, we will sink in the water that was meant for us to walk on and reach the other side. Someone may ask, "How do I overcome fear?" The only way to overcome fear is to fear God always, with reverent awe of His omniscience and omnipotence and all His magnificence. That is why the Bible says in Proverbs 9:10a, "The fear of the Lord is the beginning of wisdom…" To be awe-inspired of God is the way to overcome fear, every time we become afraid we must remind ourselves that “greater is He that is in us than he that is in the world”, and we must never forget what our portion is. 2 Timothy 1:7 says, “For God has not given us a spirit of fear, but of power and of love and of a sound mind.” May fear never be the cause of our death in stagnation; sometimes you have to make that move while afraid.

Sometimes You Have To Make That Move While Afraid

CHAPTER FIVE

INSPIRATIONAL LIFE MOVES – RECENT HISTORY

"We keep moving forward, opening new doors, and doing new things because we're curious and curiosity keeps leading us down new paths."- Walt Disney

---

Movement and history are inseparable. A study of history will be incomplete without studying the movement of people, alliances, systems, and philosophies. There have been many movements that have caught the attention of various scholars and writers throughout the history of mankind. On one hand, some movements have been unenviable, underwhelming, lackluster, and downright disappointing; on the other hand, there have been some game-changing, pioneering, exceptional, never-to be-forgotten and awe-inspiring moves since the beginning of creation. I dedicate this section to the latter kind of moves.

◆ PEOPLE WHO DARED TO MOVE

The great achievements and progress made by humanity since the beginning of time can be traced back to an individual who dared to make a move. Some of the moves came with great sacrifices, battles, opposition, and even loss of life. We can continue to draw strength and learn from all the people who refused to die in stagnation and decided that they were going to get their move on, no matter what the price might be. We look at a few individuals whose moves continue to inspire many throughout the world.

King Shaka – there are few African warriors who have a name to match King Shaka's. He was the son of a chief called Senzangakhona in the area presently called KwaZulu Natal in South Africa. This man's exploits continue to form part of folklore and history in many African communities. King Shaka established a military juggernaut of his era, which conquered everything on its path. He initiated a battle move whereby his army would approach the enemy using a U-formation. The formation used by his army enabled it to surround and overpower the enemy, and attain swift victories. The military victories and conquests had more to do with Shaka's military strategy, which was executed with precision.

King Shaka was a mover and shaker in the literal sense, he was always moving, shaking things up and conquering and expanding his empire. Like many figures in history who have opponents and supporters, King Shaka continues to draw derision from many, yet for many others, he remains an inspirational and historical figure. His movements through the Southern African landscape helped to create a renowned military force and established a strong, fearsome, and large Zulu nation. A testimony of this is that the Zulu are the largest tribal group in South Africa and IsiZulu is the most commonly spoken African language in Southern Africa today.

President Abraham Lincoln – the 16th President of the United States of America is still one of the most famous, celebrated and admired leaders in the history of humanity. He was a man of strong convictions coupled with a resolve to see those convictions to fruition. This man suffered many defeats before winning the presidential race, he had failed to be elected or appointed to positions of state speaker, legislator, senator, and congressman, yet he never gave up. He decided to make another move to run for the presidency. Many of us would not have even dared to think of being involved in any role that required voting, let alone that of POTUS.

At one point in his early life this man worked on a farm, yet after many setbacks he rose and made his greatest move which catapulted him and secured his name in the history books. One of his greatest, revolutionary and inspirational moves was perhaps to conclude and issue the Emancipation Proclamation that was a final declaration against slavery in America. His willingness to move resolutely for a good cause, especially against the tide, has ensured that history will always regard him in high esteem.

Pioneers Go Where Others Have Never Gone Before

George Washington Carver – Pioneers go where others have never gone before. To do this one requires an attitude that says, "If I fail, no one had succeeded before, if I succeed, others will be able to follow." It is with this mindset that this pioneer became the first African-American student at Iowa State University in 1891, despite many setbacks which also included refusal of entry to other universities because of his race. When he graduated, he became the first African-American to earn a Bachelor of Science degree in 1894. He took another great move by becoming the first African-American lecturer at the same university.

This son of Black slaves went on to be a respected and recognised researcher and teacher in the agricultural field. He became part of the pioneering researchers that revolutionised modern agriculture, especially the development of new crops as well as his idea of crop rotation and its benefits of improving soil productivity and sustainable yield. He went on to research and develop more than 300 products from food products, detergents, paper, cosmetics, and medicines to give a few examples. As a testimony of the man's pioneering exploits, after his death President Franklin D. Roosevelt signed a legislation for a monument to be erected in Carver's memory, an honour that was up to that time only reserved for past presidents. Today the field of scientific research has made astounding developments and this success was built on the work of pioneers like Carver who were willing to make a move into the unknown.

Madam CJ Walker – this lady suffered from hair loss which caused her unimaginable pain and shame, especially at the time in the 1910s when Black people in America still had fresh wounds that had been inflicted by centuries of slavery and disenfranchisement. In fact, her parents had just been freed as slaves, and she was their fifth child and the first one to be born in freedom. She became an orphan at the tender age of seven and had all sorts of odds that one can think of working against her. Ordinarily there were many other women who suffered the same condition of uncontrollable hair loss, and tried to cover their hair with all sorts of make shift solutions yet died inwardly of shame and low self-esteem, not Madam CJ

Walker! She decided to make a move, not just any move, but an audacious move; she started a hair product manufacturing company, which exceeded expectations in a highly hostile world. Today she is reputed to be the very first self-made female millionaire in America. Talk about making a pioneering move. Your background should never become a valid excuse to keep you in the death of stagnation, get your move on!

Dr. Martin Luther King Jr. – there are few people who have captured the imagination of the world than this colossal hero of civil rights. Dr King was born into a family of pastors, both his father and grandfather had been in ministry. He followed the same path and studied theology and also went into ministry. He could have chosen to keep his focus purely on the work in church circles but when he observed the injustices that he and his fellow African-Americans were suffering, he decided to make a move. Dr King joined the civil rights movement and was one of the foremost leaders and key figures in the demonstrations and bus boycotts of 1955-1956 during which time he was arrested, abused, his home bombed.

Your Background Should Never Become A Valid Excuse To Keep You In The Death Of Stagnation, Get Your Move On!

However, his name and face became known and he became a spokesperson, leader, and pillar of the civil rights movement. Between 1957 and 1968, Dr King is reputed to have travelled more than six million miles; talk about a man on the move! Dr King remained a hero and inspiration for all activists throughout the world, even beyond his assassination in 1968. His speech called "I have a dream" continues to bring hope to many who find themselves in hopelessness. Dr King moved boldly, his legacy continues to move many into greater heights.

President Nelson Mandela – South Africa is a country that fell victim to the ravages and indulgences of colonialism, racism, and bigotry. The Black majority had wave upon wave of oppressive White minority regimes visited upon them, with varying degrees of violence and brutality. There are men and women in this country throughout different generations who demonstrated unparalleled bravery, courage, selflessness and resolve to stand up against the might of the undemocratic regimes. When these heroes of the people are named, one name will always find a place of pride and significance in that illustrious list – Nelson Mandela. This man was born of royal blood in the rural Eastern Cape in an area called Transkei; he attended the then political activist university of Fort Hare where he studied Law.

In the 1950s, he moved to Johannesburg and there his political career flourished. The first great move that Mandela made was to join the African National Congress (ANC), and later co-found its youth wing the ANC Youth League. Through his political activism in the struggle for freedom of his people, the apartheid authorities incarcerated and assaulted him on numerous occasions. His next big move was at the famous Rivonia Treason Trial, where he gave one of the most epic declarations to ever be made by a person facing longtime imprisonment or even death. In explaining the society that he was fighting for he uttered these words "… It is an ideal which I hope to live for and to achieve. But if needs be, it is an ideal for which I am prepared to die." This is a statement of a man who saw the current status of being stuck under the yoke of apartheid as death itself. It is no wonder he titled his book The Long Walk to Freedom as his was a journey that included 27 years of imprisonment, his eventual release, leading the negotiations for a new South Africa, and finally being inaugurated as the first Black president of a democratic South Africa. Mandela knew that is was going to be "A Long Walk..." but he knew that stagnation was not an option; he kept moving ahead. History will be incomplete without a mention of his name.

President Barack Obama – if ever there was an unlikely candidate for POTUS, it has to be Barack Hussein Obama. His mother was White and from Kansas, while his father was an African from Kenya. Throughout his life Obama understood and accepted that in order to achieve greatness, he had to be willing to step out of the comforts of the family and move into the unknown. One of his books is titled The Audacity of Hope, and it takes audacious hope to take a path never travelled by anyone of your kind before.

The first big move that Obama made was to leave his career as a civil rights lawyer and academic and enter the world of politics. He could have made a successful career in law or academia, however it is clear that he did not want the deathtrap called a comfort zone. Obama navigated the perilous political waters, making his way into the senate of Illinois, and afterwards being elected to the United States Senate. His next and biggest move was to run, against all odds, for the presidency of the US. His election into office of POTUS in 2008 was the biggest achievement in the history of African-Americans and other minority groups in the US. This has been one of the most inspirational moments in history and it has inspired many to believe in and make a move on their dreams. Obama's victory reminded all of us that no dream is too big, as long as we are prepared to take the next step. To borrow from his presidential campaign of 2008, "Yes You Can", and you should make that bold move!

Time and space do not allow us to talk about all the great moves that great men and women of all hues and persuasions have made throughout history of mankind. Who could ever forget luminaries such as Alexandra the Great, William Shakespeare, Marcus Garvey, Kwameh Nkrumah, Oprah Winfrey, Michael Jordan, Mahatma Ghandi, Steve Biko, Mother Theresa, Malcolm X, Steve Jobs, Amelia Earhart, Maya Angelou, Henry Ford, Julius Nyerere, Albert Einstein, Sam Walton, Larry Page, Steve Harvey, Penny Knight, Mark Zuckerberg and the list can reach across the seas, if one were to try and include all inspirational and historical figures who made great moves. We can learn that history is shaped by people who are willing to make a move; if you want to make history, get your move on!

INSPIRATIONAL LIFE MOVES – BIBLICAL TIMES

History is incomplete without a historical account of the journey of God and mankind, and there is no better source to refer to than the Bible. It is perhaps necessary to revisit the very first book of the Bible and we read in Genesis 1:1-3; it says, 'In the beginning God created the heavens and the earth. The earth was without form, and void; and darkness was on the face of the deep. And the Spirit of God was hovering over the face of the waters. Then God said, "Let there be light"; and there was light.' This is the first ever recorded movement, when light appeared (moved in), darkness disappeared (moved out), and then followed all other forms of movement. Adam and Eve were created fully mobile, that is why Adam was given the responsibility to move around and take care of the garden. After the fall of Man to sin, we also read about God moving in the garden and it says, "And they heard the sound of the Lord God walking in the garden in the cool of the day, and Adam and his wife hid themselves from the presence of the Lord God among the trees of the garden." Ever since creation the universe, including our own planet earth, continues in movement, while we may not perceive it, the earth is orbiting the sun at a breathtaking 108 000 km/h. If, for example, the earth were to stop orbiting the sun for a few days, the imbalance that this would cause to nature would be catastrophic to a point of mass-scale loss of life. Therefore, it is safe to say movement was originally designed, created, and ordained by God.

◆ MOVES OF BIBLICAL PROPORTIONS

Biblical history records remarkable men and women who made great and often very daring moves. It would not be amiss to say the moves that they made were of Biblical proportions.

These great moves continue to inspire many in their walk of life, throughout history including the present day and to the ends of time. The Bible is essentially a book that captures various moves, voluntary, forced, unplanned, unforeseen, and accidental, and we discuss some of the people in the Bible who did get their move on.

◆ Abram

Terah lived in Ur of the Chaldeans. This man had a son called Abram, and together with Sarai his daughter-in-law and Lot his grandson by another son they set forth to move from their kinsmen. Though the intended destination was Canaan, Terah for some unknown reason instead settled with his family in the land of Haran.

After the death of Terah, in Haran, God called Abram to make a move, and we see this in Genesis 12:1. It says, “Now the Lord had said to Abram: “Get out of your country, from your family and from your father’s house, to a land that I will show you.” God went on to promise Abram that He was going to make him great and known and he was going to be a father of many nations. Incidentally and remarkably, Abram was by then 75 years old and he and his wife Sarai had no children. God renamed Abram as Abraham and Sarai as Sarah, names that meant father and mother of many nations, respectively.

Abraham made the move into the unknown, and he did this purely by having faith in the promises of God. Abraham and his wife and Lot sojourned (although he separated from them at some point) through various areas and for a good 24 years there was no sign of a child nor the settling into God's promised land. Yet Abram continued to move each time God instructed Him to, because he understood that it was necessary for him to allow God to always direct his steps; he epitomised the scripture which says, "the steps of a righteous man are directed by the Lord." Abram did not wait for God to prove or provide evidence before making a move; when God said 'go' he got his move on. God blessed Abraham and Sarah with Isaac, who was to be the father of Israel and today their descendants account for the Jewish, Christian, and Islam family throughout the world. Abraham, moved, and God was pleased with the moves and the blessings flowed and continue to flow.

History Is Shaped By People Who Are Willing To Make A Move

◆ Jacob

Isaac the son of Abraham had two sons, Esau was the older and Jacob the younger. It so happened that when Isaac was old and his eyesight failing him, he set out to bless his sons in preparation for his death. The younger son prepared an elaborate scheme to steal the blessing that was meant for the firstborn, and when the wrath of Esau was rightfully kindled, Jacob fled and went to dwell in a far place in the house of Laban, his maternal uncle. Jacob worked for Laban and with the passage of time, he fell in love with and wanted to marry Rachel, the younger of Laban's two daughters. Laban gave Jacob the condition that he had to work for seven years to earn the hand of Rachel in marriage. Jacob had tricked his father to bless him instead of Esau, and as fate would have it, he was due for some painful payback.

At the end of the seven years, the date of marriage arrived, but instead of Laban presenting Rachel to Jacob, he instead covertly sent Leah, and Jacob was then forced to marry Leah and work for another seven years to marry Rachel, his first choice. In the Sepedi language they say "molato ga o bole" meaning a debt has no expiry date, and Jacob learned this the hard way.

Movement Was Originally Designed, Created, And Ordained By God

After working for 20 years and eventually marrying Rachel, Jacob had to make a move. Often, we are forced into making a move when we suddenly encounter unforeseen hostility, this was certainly the case with Jacob as we see in Genesis 31:1-2 where it says, "Now Jacob heard the words of Laban's sons, saying, "Jacob has taken away all that was our father's, and from what was our father's he has acquired all this wealth." And Jacob saw the countenance of Laban, and indeed it was not favorable toward him as before." This must have caused Jacob great consternation, because it is never easy when people that we trusted and thought were for us suddenly change their countenance against us. However, sometimes the rejection and hostility is a nudge that it is time to get our move on.

In verse 3 of the same book, we see God giving Jacob the following instruction, "Then the Lord said to Jacob, "Return to the land of your fathers and to your family, and I will be with you." Jacob made the move and while on the way back to his hometown, in the middle of the night an angel of God appeared to him and wrestled with him the whole night. At the break of dawn, the angel wanted to leave but Jacob refused to let the angel go until he blessed him. The angel broke his hip socket in order to free himself and changed Jacob's name to Israel. This great move by Jacob, made him encounter God in a new, life-transforming and destiny- changing manner, to this day a nation is named after him as a result. To think that Jacob made this move while fearful that Esau was going to kill him makes this move much more remarkable and inspirational. Sometimes the greatest move is the scariest. Get your move on even while shaking in your boots!

◆ Joseph

Sometimes life forces us into moves that we have never predicted. Joseph was one of the sons of Israel, he and his younger brother Benjamin were the only two sons of Rachel, and there were ten other sons born of the older wife Leah. These twelve sons are the heads of the twelve tribes of Israel. Joseph's father greatly loved him, more than all the other children and he went as far as giving him a specially designed coat of many colours.

Joseph was also gifted in dreaming dreams and visions and the interpretation thereof. Favour and the ability to dream often draws opposition, criticism, jealousy, and resentment; Joseph was to learn this the hard way. His brothers hated him and they sought to do anything to remove him from their midst, whatever it would take. Joseph's brothers contemplated killing him, but eventually settled to selling him to the Ishmaelites who sold him further as a slave in Egypt, where he ended up as a servant to Potiphar, one of the captains in Pharaoh's force.

Joseph's move to Egypt was not his choice. His next move required him to make a choice and carry it out. Potiphar's wife lusted after Joseph and she tried all sorts of tricks to lure him into bed. One day she was brazen and tried to force Joseph to bed; Joseph had to make a decision at this moment. He decided to make a move and run from this temptation. Sometimes walking away is not even an option, but one has to run for dear life as destiny may depend on it. Potiphar's wife got hold of Joseph's coat as he was fleeing and used it as evidence when she laid a false accusation of rape against Joseph.

The authorities wrongfully incarcerated Joseph and he served time in jail. Joseph had interpreted dreams of two of the inmates who happened to be chief baker and the butler in the house of Pharaoh. The interpretation of the dream of the butler was that he was going to be released and restored by Pharaoh in three days; and Joseph asked this man to remember his wrongful jailing. The dream was fulfilled but when this servant was released, he forgot about Joseph, even though he had promised to remember and send him help.

At times when you find yourself in the pit of stagnation there will be people who will promise to come help you, yet they will somehow carry on with their lives and forget about their pledges. It happened with the passage of time that Pharaoh had a troubling dream which forced him to call all the trusted magicians and wise men, but none could interpret this dream. God made the ex-inmate to remember Joseph, and he was brought before Pharaoh and he interpreted the dream and what needed to happen to avoid a national disaster. Pharaoh appointed Joseph to be prime minister of Egypt, and Joseph's God given strategy to preserve food in the seven years of abundance, for later use in the seven years of famine saved Egypt. Most astoundingly, God used this to save Joseph's family from famine, including his own brothers who had betrayed him. We need to pay attention to how we treat others when God finally vindicates us; this reveals how much God can entrust us with. Remember, God never forgets a righteous move. Sometimes families, communities, even nations, are waiting for your move; do not let them die in their stagnation.

Sometimes The Rejection And Hostility Is A Nudge That It Is Time To Get Our Move On

---

◆ Ruth

Loyalty is one of the great human virtues and has rewards and benefits that can go beyond one's own lifetime. There is no greater demonstration of this than what is demonstrated in the life of a woman called Ruth. In the book of Ruth, we read about a woman named Naomi who had escaped famine in Bethlehem and resettled in Moab with her husband Elimelech and their two sons, Mahlon and Chilion. Elimelech died and left Naomi with the two sons, who eventually married Moabite women, Chilion married a lady called Orpah and Mahlon married Ruth.

Maob seems to have been a place of death for the male species, because the two sons of Naomi also died seemingly within a short space apart. Naomi set forth to return to Bethlehem as there was no reason for her to remain in Moab any longer; this is understandable considering the loss she had suffered in that place. Naomi told her two daughters-in-law that they could return to their families as she was moving back to her hometown. Orpah kissed her mother-in-law and bid her farewell, and set forth to begin a new life. Ruth responded differently and out of the norm, Ruth records her words thus, “But Ruth said, ‘Do not urge me to leave you or to return from following you. For where you go I will go, and where you lodge I will lodge. Your people shall be my people, and your God my God’.” Ruth decided that although Moab was her home, and a place where she was probably born and raised in, she decided to get her move on.

There are times when destiny calls you from the known and familiar into a place of uncertainty. Ruth made the call to forsake the known world, which was also filled with pain and heartache, she refused to die in her place of affliction and set forth in loyalty to Naomi and they set forth to Bethlehem with nothing to their names. It was because of the perfect timing of the move that Naomi and Ruth came to Bethlehem during the time of barley harvest. Due to this timely move, Ruth found herself scavenging in the field of one Boaz, and in the unlikely and unfathomable fashion, she found favour in his sight. A key lesson from Ruth’s work in the field is the reminder that before promotion, we must bow down and get our hands dirty; remember that God lifts the humble. Go down to be raised up.

Boaz admired Ruth for her loyalty to Naomi and her willingness to go where Naomi went. He eventually married Ruth, and she became the mother of Obed, who became the father of Jesse, the father of warrior King David. Ruth transitioned from losing her husband, to scavenging in a field, being married again, to being a great grandmother to a great king. This is a demonstration that God will move you from shame, then from glory to glory. Like Ruth, when you make a move with nothing but the favour of God, expect the favour of God to make something out of you.

◆ **David**

It would be impossible to discuss historical and legendary figures of the Bible yet leave out David. The son of Jesse was a shepherd, and lived under the proverbial shadow of his older brothers all his life. David did not allow his obscurity to turn him into a shadow of his God ordained true self. Circumstances must never define and confine us to permanent stagnation. David used the time in obscurity to prepare himself for any opportunity and anything that life would throw his way. It was in the so- called forgotten world of a shepherd that he killed a bear and a lion, and in doing this, he acquired the bravery of a lion. Use your time in obscurity to hone your untapped skills because when opportunities come, you will need to make your move swiftly and execute the move with skillful precision.

David was a man who made many stupendous moves, he moved swiftly to rescue a lamb from the jaws of a lion. In one epic move, he bravely went to the front lines of the battlefield, being just a teenager and killed the giant called Goliath, and in that one move rescued his people Israel from the terror of the Philistines. Considerably, David was not perfect, and some of his inglorious moves show this, like when he got a man killed in battle so that he could take his wife, a bad and evil move that we should never emulate.

The life of David was characterised by danger as the books of 1 and 2 Samuel record so vividly. It is for these reasons that David's moves were mostly in life and death situations. He had to flee from the house of King Saul when he wanted to kill him. Saul was jealous that people celebrated David for his military exploits. There will be times when you may be forced to move because you are deemed a threat to those who are your superiors, and they may seek to do you untold and irreparable harm. David lived in caves and stayed on the move continually to avoid Saul and his spies who pursued him with an insatiable appetite for violence.

David had to make an ultimate move when he faced imminent danger and there was seemingly no escape or even a chance of fighting his way out of the situation. It was during his life as an exile that David settled in a place called Ziklag and built a small community with men that had joined him in his life as a refugee. One day when David and his men had left town to go to battle, their supposed confederates turned them back, and they returned to find Ziklag burned to the ground and the women, children and all their possessions taken by the Amalekites, a marauding army that left untold misery and loss in its wake.

The men that were with David had come to him helpless and as outcasts, the Bible describes these men in this manner in 1 Samuel 22:2, “And everyone who was in distress, and everyone who was in debt, and everyone who was bitter in soul, gathered to him. And he became commander over them. And there were with him about four hundred men.” But when they found their children and women taken captive these very men turned against David and sought to stone him to death.

Life is full of such unpleasant surprises, that in times of great affliction and sorrow, the people whom you have helped may be indifferent to your plight, or they may add salt to your already painful wounds. The Bible says David encouraged himself in the Lord his God, and then he enquired of the Lord thus, in 1 Samuel 30:8, “And David inquired of the Lord, “Shall I pursue after this band? Shall I overtake them?” He answered him, “Pursue, for you shall surely overtake and shall surely rescue.” It appears that upon receiving the word from God, David was able to convince these men who had become turncoats to join him in pursuing the Amalekites. This great move based on the word from the Lord, led to David and his men overtaking and slaying the Amalekites.

Astoundingly, David and his men plundered the Amalekites and took not only what was taken from Ziklag, but much more wealth which had been taken from neighbouring areas. As long as there is still breath in you, and God’s word is still available, do not concede to premature death, get moving, spoils and treasures lie ahead.

Remember, God Never Forgets A Righteous Move

◆ The Shunammite Woman

In the book of 2 Kings, we read about the exploits and miracles of Prophet Elisha, who was anointed to succeed the great Prophet Elijah. There was a woman in Shunem, who the Bible, in 2 Kings chapter 4 simply calls the Shunammite woman; she and her husband built a chamber on the roof of their property for prophet Elisha to lodge in as he travelled around the area to do the work of God. This woman and her husband were rich and virtually needed nothing, except that they had no children. Elisha prophesied that this family was going to be blessed with a child, and the following year the Shunammite and her husband had a son.

The son grew and was healthy, until one day he cried about a headache while out in the field with his father and he was sent home to his mother who tried to nurse him but he died. The Shunammite woman had a never-say-die attitude, excuse the pun; she laid the dead child on the bed of the prophet in the upper chamber and set out to find the prophet. She had not conceded that the child was dead and she made her move, believing God for a miracle since this child was a miracle baby. She guarded her words and refused to speak death as she went to find the prophet; when her husband asked her what the matter was she said, “All is well” even when the prophet sent his servant Gehazi to meet her while she was approaching and asked what the matter was, she also said to him, “All is well”. She insisted that the prophet come with her. When he got to the home, he shut the door and prayed to God, and the child came back to life. There are times when you have to make a move in the midst of tragedy in order to try to get help even when some say it is too late.

There came a great famine in the land and the Shunammite woman left her town and settled in a foreign land for seven years, and lost everything that she owned. It happened that she returned to Shumen poor and landless, however Gehazi had been narrating the prophet's exploits and miracles to the local king including how the Shunammite woman received her son back from death, as a miracle wrought by God through Prophet Elisha. When she appeared, Gehazi recognised her and her son and pointed them out to the king. Her brazen move when the child had died, which led to the miracle of the child's resurrection, became her key to the restoration of her land and wealth, as the king instructed that she be restored all that she had lost, including the lost harvest for the past seven years. All this happened because this woman defied the defeat of death and made a move that restored the life of her son, and she was restored of all she had lost.

Go Down To Be Raised Up

◆ John the Baptist

The Old Testament of the Bible records many prophecies about the birth of the Messiah, Christ the anointed one, who was to restore the Kingdom of God and redeem the nation of

Israel. One of the prophets who prophesied extensively about the impending arrival of Christ was Isaiah. We read in Isaiah 7:14 and it says, "Therefore the Lord himself will give you a sign. Behold, the virgin shall conceive and bear a son, and shall call his name Immanuel." We also read in Isaiah 9:6 and it says, "For unto us a Child is born, unto us a Son is given; And the government will be upon His shoulder. And His name will be called Wonderful, Counselor, Mighty God, Everlasting Father, Prince of Peace."

Biblical scholars estimate that after the last words recorded in Malachi, the last book of the Old Testament, God went silent and did not speak to mankind through His servants for 400 years. The next time God spoke was through angels, to announce the birth of Jesus Christ and a man called John, both through miraculous births. John was born of Elizabeth and Zachariah who were well beyond child-bearing ages, and Jesus Christ the son born to a virgin through the immaculate conception.

John's assignment was to prepare the way and introduce the ministry of Jesus Christ on earth. In order to do this John the Baptist, as he was to be known, moved away from the comforts of his home and the religious formalities of the temple. He went to the wilderness as the scriptures show us in Matthew 3:1-2 and it says, "In those days John the Baptist came preaching in the wilderness of Judea, and saying, "Repent, for the kingdom of heaven is at hand." This move into the wilderness is arguably the most important move in the New Testament in that it set the scene and laid the foundation for the ushering in of the Gospel. Many people came to be baptised by John in the river Jordan, and he was chosen by God to also baptise Jesus Christ, the Son of God, and point out the Messiah and lead people to Him for their salvation.

John's assignment was divinely ordained, and he moved with determination and singlemindedness of purpose. He did not wear clothes that were worn by his contemporaries, he wore a garment made of a camel's skin with a leather belt, neither did he eat the regular diet but ate honey and locusts. John understood, more clearly than most of us, that you cannot rely on a system that you are trying to change, hence there is a saying that "don't bite that hand that feeds you". Sometimes to attain the promises of God, we have to move and be set apart for our assignment. A move can cause a great shift from the norm, but if you pursue a move and carry it through, it can shift the norm into the beyond normal; John the Baptist's move is a classic testimony of this. That is why Jesus Christ spoke of John the Baptist in this manner in Matthew 11:11 "Assuredly, I say to you, among those born of women there has not risen one greater than John the Baptist; but he who is least in the kingdom of heaven is greater than he." Jesus Christ is practically saying John is only lesser than Christ and no one else, what an approval! You may be the John of your industry, or neighborhood or generation, but are you willing to get your move on and usher another dimension of the Kingdom of God in your time?

Get Moving, Spoils And Treasures Lie Ahead

GREAT MOVEMENTS THAT MOVE THE WORLD

We just looked at some of the greatest and most inspirational moves by various individuals in the history of mankind. There is another form of movement in the form of great movements that have been undertaken by humanity, and these movements show the power of collaboration, congruency, and collective focus in execution. The Bible highlights the power of agreement in pursuit of any undertaking, and we see this in Amos 3:3, which says, "Can two people walk together without agreeing on the direction?" Matthew 18:19 says, "I also tell you this: If two of you agree here on earth concerning anything you ask, my Father in heaven will do it for you."

The two scriptures teach a very important principle on the hallmark of a movement involving more than one person. The principle of agreement does not only apply to endeavours that God has ordained or approved, although those that are from God and of God, He promises His blessing to see those succeed. Unfortunately, the power of the principle of agreement applies even when people agree to plan evil. We will focus on various movements that have captured the imagination of the world throughout history. The success of these movements and the duration for which they were sustained is a testimony of what can be achieved through moving in agreement.

◆ EXODUS

The children of Israel came down with their father Israel and settled in Egypt when Joseph was prime minister. Only 70 people arrived, and within a period of about four hundred years, their number had grown into millions, as the Bible records in the book of Exodus that they grew in number and filled all the land of Egypt. After about 350 years there was a new Pharaoh who did not know Joseph nor all his great works. This Pharaoh was both afraid and jealous of the Israelites or Hebrews as they were also called, and he sought to oppress them and suppress their numbers. Eventually this Pharaoh made an evil decree that all male Hebrew children be killed by being cast into the river. It is amazing how God can often use the same place that is meant to harm you to elevate you. We see this in the book of Exodus; we read about a child who was to be named Moses. He was put in a basket and hidden in the same river where Hebrew children were being drowned. To further illustrate that God works things according to his purpose, Pharaoh's daughter discovered Moses, adopted, and raised him in the palace.

Moses grew up as a Hebrew because his sister (unbeknown to Pharaoh) had been hired to raise him, and when he became a man, he chose his true family. On one visit to his people, Moses witnessed an Egyptian beating a Hebrew man, and he killed the Egyptian. When he discovered that this was known, he fled and settled in a far place called Midian, where he became a herdsman, husband and father, and he forgot the past, or so he thought.

We read one of the most jaw-dropping encounters in the Bible in Exodus 3:2; it says, "And the Angel of the Lord appeared to him in a flame of fire from the midst of a bush. So he looked, and behold, the bush was burning with fire, but the bush was not consumed." God instructed Moses to go back to Egypt to free the Israelites because their cry had reached God's ears and it was time for their deliverance. After encouragement from God, Moses made the move because he understood that some moves are restoration and restitution steps to alter the course of history. Moses went to Pharaoh and after many signs and wonders and plagues, Pharaoh said to Moses, "go, you and your people." Moses knew that he had to make the move so that the children of Israel could be finally free. This led to the great Exodus, a movement of an estimated six million people moved from Egypt on a journey to the Promised Land.

It was during this great movement that God performed great miracles such as the parting of the Red Sea and the Jordan River, healed those who were bitten by snakes, provided shelter from the elements, and demonstrated his care and made provisions to mankind. Tragically, there was rebellion, complaints and murmuring among some of the people in transit in the wilderness, and God turned what was meant to be a few weeks trip into a 40-year journey. However, because God is still faithful, He provided food and water in the wilderness and the people's clothes and shoes were never worn out for all those years. God fulfilled his promise; the people who remained in faith entered the Promised Land and dwelt therein. Today we have a book in the Bible called Exodus and this is named after this great movement of God's people.

Sometimes To Attain The Promises Of God, We Have To Move And Be Set Apart For Our Assignment

---

◆ ANTI SLAVERY MOVEMENT

There are many forms of slavery and all its forms are evil. There is a form of slavery where people are taken from their land and brought to foreign or new lands, where they are forced to toil under deplorable and inhuman conditions. Slavery, in all its despicable hues, stems purely from the greed and evil hearts of men, who believe that they are superior to others and they can therefore literally buy and sell those they deem to be inferior.

It is one thing to enslave and oppress people in their own country, it is quite another thing to forcefully remove them from their native land, and make them travel across treacherous seas, under sub-human conditions, often naked and chained together. The enslaved are finally put on public auction and sold to slave masters, with a foreign language, culture, food, in a far-off land with a different climate. The African continent, especially the western part of it, was the biggest casualty of the pandemic of slavery. Historians estimated that the trans-Atlantic slave trade dispatched more than 12 million African slaves mainly to South and North America, as well as Europe, and an estimated 2 million died in transit and their bodies were cast into the waters, buried namelessly and in ignominy in the vast seas.

The slaves that survived the perilous and cruel voyages were thrust into the harsh plantations, given new names and called Negroes, and had to perform back-breaking work with no support or care whatsoever. The slaves rose and sought justice when the burden became too heavy to bear. There comes a time in your life when you realise that without rising up your condition will never improve, instead they are set to get worse.

The anti-slavery movement was born and the slaves were willing to do whatever it took to regain their freedom even though many would have no means to return to their native lands.

This movement cost many limbs and lives, and there are many who were buried in unmarked and untraceable graves. The anti-slavery movement became a key aspect in the American Revolution and war, and something had to give eventually, as the scourge of slavery was increasingly seen in its true and vile colours. The resilience, courage and bravery of these exiled Africans, as well as the enlightenment of many who joined the cause for justice made many nations support the abolitionist movement, and those who still supported slavery became increasingly isolated. Slavery was finally abolished in the late 1800s although its remnants lasted well into the early twentieth century. Sometimes you have to move when you realise that your life is worse than death itself, because any move you make is surely better than the death of stagnation. The anti- slavery movement may not have been able to repatriate the slaves back to their native lands, but it made sure that they did not continue to die in captivity.

Some Moves Are Restoration And Restitution Steps To Alter The Course Of History

---

◆ SPACE EXPLORATION MOVEMENT

Mankind has always been curious, and this is reflected in the discoveries, innovations and inventions that continue to inspire and show the limitless possibilities that are out there. Man moved from harnessing fire to use it to heat iron and turn into various instruments, melt precious metals and turn these into jewel pieces and money, developed the steam engine and powered industrialisation. In recent years, we have seen the advancement of air travel, the internet, and wireless communication. There is no stopping; new ideas keep rolling out at a pace that is almost impossible to keep up with. There is a continuation of wave upon wave of innovative and inventive movement.

In the 1950s, the space exploration movement captured the imagination of the world. The space programme as we know it was an audacious endeavour to explore the universe beyond the earth's atmosphere. Man wanted to see what lay out there in the vast expanse called the universe and the far galaxies. The space exploration movement was revolutionised by the development of rockets that were able to launch satellites into space, the first of these were in the 1950s. Satellite communication technology took technology to unprecedented heights, both literally and figuratively. This technology allowed scientists to study the earth and be able to predict weather patterns as well as the advent of phenomena such as typhoons and hurricanes.

The satellite opened up the endless possibility of telecommunications. In the early years of the Cold War, America and the Soviet Union were the main antagonists, and they sought to outwit each other and see who could conquer space first. The Soviets were the first to launch the first artificial satellite into space in 1957; the Americans launched their first satellite into space in early 1958. In 1961 and 1962, the Soviets and Americans both succeeded in sending men into space. Furthermore, they were the first to orbit the earth successfully.

The culmination of these early days of the race beyond the galaxies was the first moon landing by the Americans in 1969 as part of the Apollo Mission. One of the most historic and famous words were uttered by Astronaut Neil Armstrong when he landed on the moon, he said, “That’s one small step for man, one giant leap for mankind.”

Due to the space exploration movement, there were further advancement in communications technology, with satellite television, cellular communications, satellite imagery to assist in times of fires, floods and even in agriculture, to name a few examples. It is safe to say that science and technological advancement owe a great gratitude to the space exploration movement that was willing to take the risk of breaking beyond the earthly boundaries. There is now a new way of tourism- space tourism- where companies are allowing people to spend some time in space, if you have a few million dollars to spare for such an outing. Your move might not be inter-galactical; however, it can definitely go beyond man-made and self-made boundaries and restrictions. Move and explore, you may discover new and untapped possibilities!

Any Move You Make Is Surely Better Than The Death Of Stagnation

---

◆ SOCIAL MEDIA MOVEMENT

There is a region in California in the US called Silicon Valley; for years, this area has been the hub and melting pot of computer and related technologies. It is no accident that some of the foremost technology startups were birthed in this region. There are many technology start- ups that have gone bust, especially during the infamous crash after the dot.com bubble of the early 2000s, which was precipitated mainly by the nightmare that was known as Y2K. The scary phenomenon called Y2K was a fancy acronym for Year 2000, which had most speculating that when the world moved from 1999 to 2000 computer-based systems would crash and disrupt the world as we knew it. In preparation for Y2K many companies and individuals had invested heavily in tech companies. The massive investments lifted the share prices and these tech companies were extremely overcapitalised. Needless to say the world did not only survive Y2K, but moved into even greater levels of computers and related technological developments.

Social media is one of the pioneering inventions of the post Y2K era. It is no surprise that the definition of social media is listed in the Oxford Dictionary as "Websites and applications that enable users to create and share content or to participate in social networking." The social media movement is said to have gained momentum with the advent of blogging around 1999, and some of the key developments include, platforms like LinkedIn and MySpace around 2003, YouTube in 2005, Facebook and Twitter in 2006, and in later years, Instagram, WhatsApp, Minds.Com, Gab, and TikTok, and the list continues to grow unabated.

It is therefore hardly surprising that the social media movement has grown so much and it is continuing to infiltrate all areas of our lives; this is because human beings were created to socialise and communicate with one another. Throughout history and in all societies humans have used various forms of gatherings and communication channels to satisfy the need to stay in touch and connect with others. The era we live in is the busiest and most hectic, and this is compounded by rapid urbanization, which adds other time-consuming aspects to life such as traffic, multiple jobs, and what are called side hustles and this is increasingly squeezing out time from the unchanging 24 hours we each are allocated by God daily.

The need to socialise and relate to others is part of our DNA and sanity and this and time constraints presented us with a problem. While we were trying to figure out a solution, then entered the social media movement with the technology that allows connectivity. Its beauty is that brings people together even though they are physically in different places, at times countries, and continents.

There are downsides to social media such as inadvertently encouraging people not to prioritise real-life physical contact and the fact that families spend more time on social media than with those they live with under the same roof. Nevertheless, no one can deny the power of social media in shaping the world and allowing trends and ideas to move from one country and continent to the world in a matter of seconds. Sometimes you need to identify a need, then create a solution to address that need and then move swiftly to introduce the solution; you may contribute to shaping the world and profit from your idea.

◆ ARAB SPRING MOVEMENT

Post-colonial Africa seems to have largely inherited the strong-arm techniques and tendencies of their former colonial masters. This led to a monster often referred to as the "Big-men Syndrome". This refers to political figures who consider themselves above reproach and who do not see the need to account to the electorate, hence they are able to go against the wishes of the voters; they assume power and cling to it by any means necessary. This is often exacerbated by the support that these politicians receive from their big-men clubs in their regional blocs as well as the gap-toothed, and sometimes complicit African Union. A combination of these factors together with tribal and political fault lines, the invisible hand of some western and eastern powers, and the ever-present danger of war, disease, low literacy levels, as examples, have collectively hampered the development of many African states. The biggest obstacle to Africa's progress is the big men, as most, if not all the other contributors to Africa's stagnation stem from the big men's misrule and maladministration.

Contrary to popular belief, the problems of despots and misrule were not unique to sub-Saharan Africa; the factors that ignited the Arab Spring movement serve as evidence. In December 2010, a man in Tunisia called Mohammed Bouazizi set himself alight; this was in protest to being refused an operating permit for his informal trading stall by the authorities. This trigged a movement that started in Tunisia in 2010, when the people (mostly young men and women), revolted against an increasingly undemocratic state, in a country where the standard of living was deteriorating and the economic performance was lackluster.

The unique feature of the Arab Spring movement is that it was one of the first mass movements to use the power of social media to spread the message, and to mobilise people in different areas and strata of society. This movement culminated with president Zine El Abidine Ben Ali being deposed in January 2011, after his 23-year long iron-fisted rule.

This movement spread into a series of large-scale pro-democracy protests across North Africa, in countries such as Algeria, Morocco, Egypt, Libya, and Sudan; as well as to some of the Middle East countries. The movement lasted two years, ending officially in 2012, and it left in its wake regime changes in Tunisia, Egypt, and Libya. The movement did not achieve all its desired results, especially when one looks at its aftermath of war, destruction, and economic collapse in countries such as Syria, Libya, and Yemen. Similarly, some of the countries like Egypt have failed to establish a democratic state. There is however no denying the scale and reach of the Arab Spring movement and how it reignited the struggle for democracy, equality, and human rights. It also served as a reminder that governments are supposed to serve at the pleasure and behest of the people, and not the other way round.

◆ BLACK LIVES MATTER MOVEMENT

The USA has not covered itself in glory when it comes to the violence that it often inflicts upon minority groups, such as

African-Americans, Hispanics, Mexicans, American-Indians, and other racial groups. There is the scourge of racial profiling by police and the targeting and inflicting abuses on minority groups; a blight on America as the country often presents itself as the paragon of democracy, equality, and the upholding of human rights. The biggest tragedy is that the police and other law enforcement agencies perpetrate some of the violence. Some of the brutality has led to premature deaths, where some young people's lives have been snuffed out with seemingly no care in the world, and more tellingly with little or no consequences for the culprits.

Often the minority groups are left with no option but to take to the streets in mass protests, which coincidentally and ironically draws the ire of the same law enforcement agencies, and more violence and brutality is meted out to the aggrieved and unarmed. An African American man called Rodney King was brutally assaulted by four White police officers after a high-speed chase by the police, and this violence was captured on video. This incident took place in Los Angeles in 1991. The acquittal of the policemen led to mass demonstrations mainly across Los Angeles; the police and army were unleashed on the protestors, and the senseless violence that followed resulted in more than 50 deaths, more than 2000 injuries and arrests; what a tragedy!

It appears as the saying goes, "the more things change, the more they stay the same," as America continues to make unpleasant headlines with racially motivated police brutality. There are movements that are sparked by an urgency for radical change and reform, some of these movements are sparked by tragic events; the Black Lives Matter (BLM) movement is one such example. The events of a tragic fatal shooting of 17 year-old Trayvon Martin, and the subsequent acquittal of the shooter named George Zimmerman led to the unplanned formation of the BLM movement. BLM is a social advocacy and protest movement that stands against racial discrimination and the cheapening of Black lives in America, and lately across the world.

In its own words, the movement is now "committed to struggling together

and to imagining and creating a world free of anti-Blackness, where every Black person has the social, economic, and political power to thrive". It is therefore not surprising that the barbaric, unfortunate, and tragic killing in Minneapolis of George Floyd by a White police officer called Derek Chauvin has led to the movement taking up the cudgels and fighting for justice and the recognition of Black lives as lives that do matter.

It is estimated that more than 15 million people protested in America in response to the call by the BLM to raise voices against this brutal death, where Floyd died with the knee of the police officer on his neck, struggling for breath and whispering, "I can't breathe". The movement has adopted the bended knee and raised fist as a symbol of solidarity for Black lives across the world. This movement has been visible and we have felt its presence in sports, media, politics, business, and other areas of life. Its reach and impact has led to some sporting codes and teams including the Black Lives Matter emblem in their kits, adverts and communiques, and this is testimony of its growing stature and hopefully a prelude to true equality for the Black race across the world.

This movement has picked up and is carrying forward the baton that was in the hands of the social justice and political activists like Marcus Garvey, Booker T. Washington, W.E.B Du Bois, Martin Luther King Jr, Nelson Mandela, and many other activists for matters of Black Lives. Some of these icons paid the ultimate price by losing their lives for the cause. The BLM movement does not want the lives and deaths of these icons to be in vain. Sometimes we have to make a move and refuse to stand indifferently in the face of injustice. If it moves your heart, get moving!

Move And Explore, You May Discover New And Untapped Possibilities!

◆ THE GOSPEL OF CHRIST

Humanity has never seen nor experienced any movement with a reach, impact, and magnitude as the Gospel of the Lord Jesus Christ. The Bible reveals the journey of man with God, through different periods and dispensations. Some of the dispensations include, the creation of Adam and Eve and their dwelling in the Garden of Eden; Noah and the rebuilding after the flood; the time of the Patriarchs (Abraham, Isaac, Israel and his 12 sons); the relocation to Egypt; Moses and the Exodus and dwelling in the Promised Land; the period of the Judges (e.g. Deborah, Gideon, Abimelech, Samson); the kings during different periods, before and after captivity and exile (e.g. Saul, David, Solomon, Josiah, Zedekiah); and the various eras of the prophets (e.g. Samuel, Elijah, Elisha, Isaiah, Jeremiah, Malachi).

The different periods and dispensations all reveal a common thread that since the fall of man in the Garden of Eden, it was not possible for humanity to walk in full righteousness and perfection before God. The scriptures also provide a shadow of the Messiah, through the need for sacrifice of animals such as bulls, sheep, and goats, to atone for transgressions as well as to be reconciled with God. The prophet Isaiah speaks in this manner about the Messiah, Jesus Christ, in Isaiah 53:5, "But He was wounded for our transgressions, He was bruised for our iniquities; the chastisement for our peace was upon Him, and by His stripes we are healed." The blood of animals was not able to offer a permanent atonement, and neither was it able to give eternal life. As a result, God unveiled His plan for salvation as seen in John 3:16 as a fulfilment of what the prophets had been speaking about, and in His own Words Jesus Christ says, "For God so loved the world that He gave His only begotten Son, that whoever believes in Him should not perish but have everlasting life."

Jesus Christ chose Himself 12 disciples whom He called Apostles, and went about all Judea and surrounding areas doing good, teaching, healing the sick, delivering those who were possessed of demons, raising the dead, and ushering the Kingdom of God. The works and words of Jesus Christ caused Him great opposition and persecution, and the Jewish religious leaders and their accomplices put him on trial. They subjected him to scourging and humiliation. Eventually they crucified him on the cross in Golgotha, and buried him in a tomb. The prophecies, including through Jesus Himself, were again fulfilled when God raised Him up on the third day. Many witnesses saw him over a period of 40 days, where He was preparing the disciples for His ascension to heaven.

In His final words before ascending to God the Father, Jesus Christ told His disciples that they must go and wait in Jerusalem to receive power through the Holy Spirit and thereafter go to all the ends of the earth to preach the Gospel and to teach and baptise those who believe. The disciples went and waited in Jerusalem in the Upper Room, and this is what happened, on the day when power was released upon the disciples; in Acts 2:4 we read that "And they were all filled with the Holy Ghost, and began to speak with other tongues, as the Spirit gave them utterance." From that moment on the Apostles set forth to preach the Gospel of Jesus Christ to different regions, in Jerusalem and surrounding areas as well as other regions as far as Europe, Africa and Asia, with God testifying for them through miracles, signs, and wonders.

There is a man who became one of the greatest disciples and Apostles of the Gospel. This man was Saul of Tarsus (who became Paul) who was prosecuting the early church of Christ until this encounter with the resurrected and ascended Jesus, we read in Acts 9:3-6, "As he journeyed he came near Damascus, and suddenly a light shone around him from heaven. Then he fell to the ground, and heard a voice saying to him, "Saul, Saul, why are you persecuting Me?" And he said, "Who are You, Lord?" Then the Lord said, "I am Jesus, whom you are persecuting. It is hard for you to kick against the goads." So he, trembling and astonished, said, "Lord, what do You want me to do?" Then the Lord said to him, "Arise and go into the city, and you will be told what you must do."

He followed the instructions and God commissioned him to preach the Gospel and plant churches in different parts of the world. While the synoptic Gospel books provide an account of what it was like to walk with Christ while He was on earth, the epistles of the Apostle Paul provide guidance on how to live with and walk with Christ in the form of the Holy Spirit. God used Paul to provide a deeper understanding of the power of the grace of God, that Jesus Christ has made available to all believers by the working of the Holy Spirit.

Many of the Apostles and disciples that followed the teaching faced and continue to face persecution, hostility, imprisonment and at times death, all because they chose to live for the Lord Jesus Christ. Amidst all the persecution, hatred, and opposition, the Gospel of Jesus Christ has reached all continents of the earth and some of the remotest villages in far corners of the earth. An estimated 2,4 billion people or 31% of the world's 7,79 billion population identify themselves as Christians or followers of Christ; as at 2020 Christianity continues to be the largest religion in the world. Ephesians

6:15 tells us, “And with your feet fitted with the readiness that comes from the gospel of peace.” We need to get our feet moving, and bring the Gospel to every place we go to, everyone needs salvation through Christ, and we are the ones who are sent.

If It Moves Your Heart, Get Moving!

CHAPTER SIX

ON THE MOVE? EXPECT OPPOSITION!

"Don't dwell on what went wrong. Instead, focus on what to do next. Spend your energies on moving forward toward finding the answer." - Denis Waitley

---

Sir Isaac Newton is a world-renowned mathematician, and he is one of the most esteemed and foremost scientists in history. He is responsible for many theories and laws that have advanced the world of science, including the law of gravity. There is a famous saying, which in fact is Newton's Third Law which states that "for every action, there is an equal and opposite reaction." This tells us that the distinguished scientist is advising us that it is not possible to move and not face any opposition, anytime there is movement, we must expect opposition. The opposition can be bold and confrontational or subtle and even underhanded, but movement will inevitably draw opposition; opposition will mostly come from external forces but some of this opposition can be from within ourselves. It is much easier to overcome the external forces than to overcome the voice of the inner man.

Part of Newton's First Law states that a body at rest has a force that is still exerted on it, even while it remains at rest. However, for a

GET YOUR MOVE ON body or object to move, there must be a larger or greater force that overcomes the force that is keeping the body stuck; this is explained through Newton's Second Law. The point is not to labour on sciences and mathematical theories and concepts, but these help us understand what we will encounter when we get our move on. Let us explore some of the sources of opposition to the moves that we intend to make.

Movement Will Inevitably Draw Opposition

◆ OPPOSITION OF THE INDEPENDENCE MOVEMENT

Africa is the richest continent in mineral resources; God in His infinite wisdom created it that way. Sadly, this natural endowment has caught the attention of all sorts of people including professional thieves and conmen; some of them were born and bred on the continent. To forge an agreement to end a contestation of European powers over Africa,

Bismarck called the Berlin Conference of November 1884 to February 1885; it was in this period that the phenomenon known as The Scramble for Africa gained traction. This was after the European nations had squabbled among themselves, about which part of Africa to annex for themselves, as though Africa were some vast open land with no owner.

At the end of this conference, countries such as Britain, France, Belgium, Portugal, and Germany laid claim to various countries across the continent. Colonialism was officially born, for the subsequent 72 years these colonial powers took over Africa, and exploited her people and resources to sustain the European nations. The only African country that was spared the colonial shackles was Ethiopia, after she fought and prevailed against Italy who had set to colonise her.

Any people who are disenfranchised, plundered, and oppressed will petition for some leniency, if that fails they will raise their voices in protest, if all else fails they will rise in a revolution. History has many lessons of these patterns, and it was a matter of time before these could play themselves out in colonial Africa, as the greed and grand theft of the colonisers went into overdrive with each passing decade. The revolution for independence gained momentum in the 1940s, and this was also a time when the world was realigning after the Second World War. The independence movement gained strength, visibility, credibility, and solidarity of purpose after it was formalised after the 5th Pan African Congress that was held in 1945.

It was after this formalisation that there was collaborative and concerted effort to push for independence across the continent. The colonial power used every available avenue and means, often with force to oppose the independence movement. In the face of hostility and at times war with the colonial powers, the Africans pressed on and were able to gain their independence, and the results of the resilience are shown in the statistics that reveal that between 1950 and 1970 about 40 countries had gained independence or some form of autonomy. 1960 was the seminal and most glorious year in this struggle as in that year alone 17 countries gained their independence.

The independence movement produced ordinary activists, courageous guerrillas, intellectual visionaries, and inspirational Pan Africanists. Some of the luminaries of the independence movement include Ghana's Kwame Nkrumah, Guinea's Ahmed Sékou Touré, Léopold Sédar Senghor of Senegal, Modibo Keita of Mali, Kenya's Jomo Kenyatta, Hastings Banda, Robert Mugabe, Thomas Sankara, Patrice Lumumba, and Kenneth Kaunda to name a few. This movement also inspired and gained intellectual vigour through some of the most esteemed African writers such as Chinua Achebe, Bessie Head, Ousmane Sembéne, Ayi Kwei Armah, Wole Soyinka, Es'kia Mphahlele, Frantz Fanon, and Ngugi wa Thiong'o, to name a few. Africans made unprecedented gains in terms of identity, national pride, and quest for freedom, and all these and more are testimony to the independence movement's persistence, because freedom is rarely ever given on a platter.

Post-independence Africa has not entirely covered itself in collective glory. Some of the luminaries betrayed the revolution, and this is demonstrated in the regression through coups, ascendency of despotic rulers, violation of human rights, incessant wars, corruption, and under-investment in infrastructure, education, and health care. Granted, external and invisible hands of those who want to continue to exploit Africa's natural resources sponsor some of the problems, however it is saddening that most of Africa's woes are self-inflicted.

Freedom Is Rarely Ever Given On A Platter

As Africans, we need to rise and make a move to reclaim the continent and ensure that it occupies its rightful place in the world. To this day, there continues to be exerted pressure against the total freedom and liberation of Africans, especially from an economic point of view. No matter how noble or successful a movement can be, it will draw opposition. Africans on the continent and in the diaspora, make a move to lift our land.

◆ OPPOSITION OF THE CIVIL RIGHTS MOVEMENT

The struggle for independence in Africa was mutually supportive to the Civil Rights Movement in the USA. African-Americans had been in the struggle for equal rights and liberties since the abolition of slavery, however there were little gains from that struggle. In the early 1950s the people began to organise themselves with increased coordination, consolidated effort, and common purpose, in what is now famously called the Civil Rights Movement.

This movement touched all areas of Black society, from issues of schooling, social infrastructure, healthcare, economic inclusion and participation, as well as being afforded the same rights and freedoms as the other communities. The biggest spark to ignite a full-scale uprising was the incident of Rosa Parks on a bus in Montgomery Alabama, on 1 December 1955. This was at a time when there was still racial segregation on buses and many public amenities in various states. It happened that the bus was full when three White men boarded, and the bus driver instructed Rosa Parks and other Black passengers to stand and cede their seats to the White men. Rosa Parks, with poise and dignity, refused to heed the instruction, and she was arrested. Her arrest sparked wide-scale protests and these turned into a formal activation of the Civil Rights Movement.

The work and unwavering efforts of the Civil Rights movement led to the abolition of many of the racist laws including racial segregation in buses and public amenities, acceptance of all races at all schools, freedom to live in any area of one's choice. Although there were many gains achieved, especially from a legislative and legal point of view, African- Americans and other minority groups continued to be subjected to racism in many areas of their daily lives.

The pressure continued to mount against all forms of racism, and one of the most well-known protests in the world was led by the Civil Rights Movement in Washington DC on 23 August 1963. It had many leaders of the movement and support from all races, and more than 200 000 people descended on the capital of the US on that momentous day. The key demand from this march was that there should be equal access to employment and job equality for everyone. It was at this march where Martin Luther King, Jr made the famous "I have a dream" speech and finally established himself as a world icon of freedom fighters. The Civil Rights Movement produced renowned leaders and activists such as Rosa Parks, Malcom X, Harriet Tubman, Sojourner Truth, Whitney Young Jr, John Lewis and many others.

May Your Move Serve As A Path And Pattern For Others To Take A Leaf From, Even When All Forces Are Working Against You

---

There continued to be a concerted push for full civil rights, but there was an equal and often brutal push back from those who wanted to exercise racial, economic, and political hegemony. Many activists paid with life and limb to withstand the unceasing onslaught. To this day, many social justice movements continue to draw lessons, strength, courage, and inspiration form the Civil Rights Movement. May your move serve as a path and pattern for others to take a leaf from, even when all forces are working against you.

◆ OPPOSITION OF THE TIANANMEN SQUARE MOVEMENT

China is one of the countries that had adopted communism in the post- World War 2 period. Mao Zedong officially inducted the People's Republic of China as a communist republic. Those who oppose communism often cite its unpalatable record when it comes to human rights, as some of the repressive regimes in history have been communist.

We learned in the previous section that human beings have always found it in their hearts to fight any form of oppression and injustice. It is for this reason that even under the most brutal regimes in the world, there are uprisings and protests of varying magnitude, with some being sporadic and others more intense and sustained. China has had a fair share of various forms of unrest and uprisings, and the government has responded heavy handedly to suppress each of these actions.

In 1989, the world witnessed the Tiananmen Square Movement. This was a large-scale protest of mainly young people, composed mostly of students. The young people had grown tired of living under the repressive arm of the regime, and they marched to demand democracy, free speech as well as freedom of the press, and other associated freedoms. The authorities killed one Hu Yaobang, a man who used to be part of the ruling party but had been expelled due to his pro-reform inclinations. In mourning Hu's death, young people, and many others who joined them, marched and took their protest to Tiananmen Square in Beijing.

Like any movement that seeks to bring any form of change, the government opposed this movement. The demands that the movement was making were a threat to the stranglehold that the Chinese regime had over the populace. The demonstrators continued to meet on Tiananmen Square in May of 1989 and the numbers kept growing each day, with an estimated one million marchers. One of the unique and courageous features of this movement was the night vigils where protestors would stay overnight on the square, a feature that was later adopted by some of the Arab Spring protests. This was despite the fact that the regime had attempted to thwart the movement by declaring martial law and releasing 250 000 troops into Beijing.

The climax of the protest was on 4th of June. The protest was met with untold violence by government forces, who opened fire on the marchers from 01h00 in the morning of that day. A war was unleashed in opposition to this movement of a largely unarmed group of marchers and in the aftermath, hundreds of people are reported to have been massacred and more than 10 000 arrested. This was a great movement and it faced a great level of opposition and resistance which led to loss of life.

One of the most iconic pictures that stands as a symbol of the resilience and bravery of freedom fighters is that of a man who stood alone in front of a military tanker (with two others behind it) and not willing to move out of its way. This man was willing to be run over by the tanker or to be shot dead on that spot; this man withstood the might of the army because he understood that any great move would be greatly opposed. Today the world knows him as "Tiananmen Square Tank Man", and his image is etched in world's collective memory. In the face of opposition, be more emboldened to get your move on.

In The Face Of Opposition, Be More Emboldened To Get Your Move On

---

◆ OPPOSITION OF THE JERUSALEM WALL-REBUILDING MOVEMENT

The Israelites experienced various waves of sieges and periods of exile. In the book of Nehemiah, we read the following account from one of the difficult times; Nehemiah 1 reads, "And they said to me, "The remnant there in the province who had survived the exile is in great trouble and shame. The wall of Jerusalem is broken down, and its gates are destroyed by fire." This was an answer when Nehemiah asked how the Jews who had survived and returned from exile were coping in Jerusalem. In Biblical and other historical times, when people were taken captive their cities or towns would be razed to the ground and left in ruins. The walls of Jerusalem were still in the state they were left in when the Israelites were taken into exile as slaves of the Babylonian empire.

The status report troubled Nehemiah greatly, and he fasted and mourned for many days. At this time, Nehemiah was the cupbearer (attendant who served in the royal courts) to the king Artaxerxes of Persia, and the king noticed and enquired about the cause of Nehemiah's countenance. Nehemiah narrated the story of how the city of his fathers lay in ruins, and he also expressed his wish to go and rebuild the walls around the city. The king heeded Nehemiah's request and he gave him letters and other documents to assist him to get help for this rebuilding project. Nehemiah got his move on and began to organise the beginning of the rebuilding project.

The trouble began when Nehemiah started to rebuild the broken walls, and he and his team faced concerted barrage of opposition. Their nemesis tried all manner of confrontation and schemes to stop the move to rebuild the city walls. The Bible records how they first mocked the rebuilding effort to discourage Nehemiah and his co-workers. In one of the statements, the spoil spots threw this shade (to borrow young people's lingo), in Nehemiah 4:3, we read, "Tobiah the Ammonite was beside him, and he said, "Yes, what they are building - if a fox goes up on it he will break down their stone wall!" When such disparaging remarks failed to deter Nehemiah, he was threatened with violence and even death.

He and his men had to build, watch, and be ready for any attack, the Bible says at one stage they had to hold a building tool with one hand and a weapon in the other hand; unheard of! When all else failed Nehemiah's adversaries tried to set a trap to harm him, and invited him to come meet them in a certain place. He gave them one of the best answers anyone could have crafted, we see this exchange in Nehemiah 6:2-3, where it says, "Sanballat and Geshem sent to me, saying, "Come and let us meet together at Hakkephirim in the plain of Ono." But they intended to do me harm. And I sent messengers to them, saying, "I am doing a great work and I cannot come down. Why should the work stop while I leave it and come down to you?" These opponents of the great move were persistent as they made this same invitation four times, and received the same answer each time.

You may have some opponents who are lying dormant until you get your move on; this is reminiscent of crocodiles that lie motionless like a tree in a river, waiting for prey to innocently step into the water. When you make a big move, there will be major opposition, some may try to discourage you, distract you, threaten you, or even set up traps to derail your plan. Acknowledge and know the opposition, but do not entertain their schemes, stay on track in your great move! While working on your move refuse to abandon the mission, no matter what the opponents say or do.

While Working On Your Move Refuse To Abandon The Mission, No Matter What The Opponents Say Or Do

---

◆ OPPOSITION OF THE EXODUS

The Exodus that we read about in the previous section is a miracle on many fronts and levels. This movement faced opposition even before it began, as Moses learned from when God appeared to him through the burning bush, in Exodus 1:19, God said to Moses, "But I am sure that the king of Egypt will not let you go, no, not even by a mighty hand." God did reassure Moses however that after all the opposition that he was going to encounter, Pharaoh would eventually relent. God showed Moses signs and miracles to confirm that He was with Him and would deliver the Hebrews from bondage.

The Bible records nine requests that Moses made to Pharaoh to release the Hebrews, and each time Pharaoh opposed and rejected the request. That was the stubbornness and hardness of Pharaoh's heart. Each time Pharaoh opposed the move of the people of God, the Lord would send a plague upon the Egyptians. The first miracle that Moses performed before Pharaoh was when Aaron dropped his rod on the ground and it became a snake. Pharaoh called his magicians to do the same, but the snake from Aaron's rod swallowed all the magicians' snakes. When you make a move, those who oppose you may do a counterfeit move to stop you, trust your move and it will thwart and overcome the adversary's counter move.

Pharaoh refused to let God's people go, and in response, God unleashed the first plague, which was the turning of the Nile River and all the water in Egypt to blood, killing all the fish in the process. Still Pharaoh opposed the move of the Hebrews, and this went on, request after request, and plague after plague but each time Pharaoh refused to release the children of God. There may be places where you are in bondage, and this is reflected in how you are treated and the balance of the relationship or agreement.

If you are giving more of you than what you receive back, it should be based on your act of love, not that you are being exploited for someone else's gain. When unsure check the nature of the relationship and whether the sacrifices that you are making are voluntary or they are a result of manipulation or threats. At times, people may promise to release you after certain conditions or goals have been met, only to shift the goal posts when that time has come. This happened with Moses and Pharaoh; each time Pharaoh would renege on his promise to free the Hebrews.

The tenth and final plague had to exceed all the others and was at an unprecedented level, and this was to ensure that Pharaoh was going to see how costly it was to keep captive those that God has already freed. We read about this plague in Exodus 11:4-5. It reads: "Then Moses said, "Thus says the Lord: 'At midnight I am going out into the midst of Egypt, 5 and all the firstborn in the land [the pride, hope, and joy] of Egypt shall die, from the firstborn of Pharaoh who sits on his throne, to the firstborn of the slave girl who is behind the hand-mill, and all the firstborn of cattle as well." There was great wailing in Egypt when all the male first born of the Egyptians families and that of their livestock died. Pharaoh's resolve was finally broken; he relented and let the people go.

The Hebrews left Egypt and travelled until they arrived at the Red Sea. Pharaoh in his stubbornness decided that he was going to pursue them, even after all the tragic plaques he had witnessed. The chariots of Egypt descended upon the Hebrews, and now they were stuck between the vast sea and

Pharaoh's chariot-riding machine. God instructed Moses to stretch his hand and point his rod to the sea, and the sea parted and made a dry path for the Hebrews to cross on. When the Egyptians army gave chase, God instructed Moses to point at the sea again, and the water came down and drowned the opponents of God's ordained move.

When you have made a great move, some people can go to great lengths to tarnish and bring your name into disrepute; it is all normal. A great move causes a great shake up, do not let this draw you back into stagnation. Stay focused on where you are going, as the past is only a place of reflection and learning and not a place of dwelling.

The Past Is Only A Place Of Reflection And Learning And Not A Place Of Dwelling

---

◆ OPPOSITION OF DAVID'S ASCENDENCY TO THE THRONE

King David had by far the most perilous journey to the throne than any other king we can read about in the Bible. It started in his father Jesse's house, where the young David was given the lowly-regarded job of a shepherd for the family's sheep. In the book of 1 Samuel we read about how the prophet Samuel was sent by God to Jesse's house to anoint the next king of Israel, after God rejected King Saul because of his rebellion and evil heart. When the prophet Samuel asked to see Jesse's sons so that he could anoint the one God had chosen as king, the brothers passed before Samuel and he saw Eliab with a well-built structure and thought that must be the one, fortunately God stopped that error.

God Will Stop Everything To Ensure That Your Opportunity Meets With You

---

After everyone had paraded themselves before the prophet, he asked this question in 1 Samuel 16:11; it reads, "Then Samuel said to Jesse, "Are all your sons here?" Jesse replied, "There is still one left, the youngest; he is tending the sheep." Samuel said to Jesse, "Send word and bring him; because we will not sit down [to eat the sacrificial meal] until he comes here." Jesse had seemingly discounted David as the potential king; that is why he waited for the question before explaining that David was missing from his siblings. Samuel said no one was to sit down until David arrived. God will stop everything to ensure that your opportunity meets with you. David eventually arrived and Samuel anointed him as the next king of Israel.

David entered the palace and ruled! That is not how it happened, although one would have expected that to be the next move. Instead, after being anointed he was sent back to tend the sheep out in the field again. It so happens that the Philistines set themselves for battle against the army of Israel, and David's brothers were also conscripted for this war and they were on the battlefield where the battle lines had been drawn. Jesse called on David to go deliver provisions to his brave and gallant brothers, at least that was what the father thought; he did not know that his sons and the entire host of the army of Israel were being terrorised by a giant called Goliath from the enemy camp. When David arrived on the scene and started asking questions, his brothers rebuked him and said he was there to watch the battle because in their view he was a mischievous youth. Sometimes when you make a great move some people will oppose you and misunderstand your assignment, David did not come to watch the battle; instead, he came to bring victory.

David slayed Goliath, and went on to become a great warrior in the Israel army and Saul's armour bearer. Because God had anointed him and

Lord was with him, David delivered many victories for the nation of Israel to a point where songs were composed about him. In 1 Samuel 18:7 we see these lyrics, "The women sang as they played and danced, saying, "Saul has slain his thousands, and David his ten thousands", and this drew the Saul's ire, and he became jealous of David and wanted him killed.

When we receive praises, we should expect some opposition, or even being despised by others, this can be useful to keep us grounded and not puffed up. The throne looked increasing unattainable for David as he had to run for his life, both literally and figuratively. Because Saul feared David and was also jealous of him, he attempted to kill him on two occasions with a spear. It was Jonathan, the son of Saul, who helped David escape, because Jonathan loved David. When you are moving up, there may be people who are insecure and they will feel threatened, and even try to discredit you; but when your great move is led by God, He will always send you help, and often this help will come from the people you least expect to assist you.

Often This Help Will Come From The People You Least Expect To Assist You

---

David received help at all the right times and in the right manner; on a few occasions, Jonathan warned him on how and when to escape. Michal, a daughter of Saul's who was married to David, also helped David to escape as she put a doll in his bed and claimed that he was sick. When David dwelt in caves and in the bush, while Saul and his men were in hot pursuit, David continued to receive help. At one time, he was hungry and was given the shewbread by the priest Ahimelech in the temple, bread which was strictly reserved for a priest; he had no weapon and the priest gave him Goliath's sword which was also in the table.

At another time, David asked the King of Moab to safeguard his parents in his homestead, until David could see what the Lord had planned for him. While he was a fugitive, David was joined by skillful and ambidextrous warriors, and this helped his cause greatly. There are a few times when Saul was about to corner David but each time God interrupted Saul's plans and he had to hastily return home. David received all this help because of what we read in 1 Samuel 18:14 which says, "David acted wisely and prospered in all his ways, and the Lord was with him." David eventually made the greatest move after all these trials and tribulations, and he ascended the throne that God had set aside for him. He ruled over Israel for 40 years, and during his reign no enemy could defeat him, and he handed the reigns to his son King Solomon. When you move in wisdom and in the fear of the Lord, no matter how great the opposition, God will be with you just like he was with David, and in all your movements, He will keep you safe from harm.

Even Against Great Opposition Keep Moving When It Is Time

◆ OPPOSITION OF PAUL'S MINISTRY

The Apostle Paul is the reason why people refer to moments of radical and dramatic change in their ways or lives as a "Damascus moment". This is based on Paul's conversion from persecuting the church of Jesus Christ, to becoming a fervent and passionate disciple and Apostle of Jesus Christ. I dwelt on this in the previous chapter. Something in the scriptures reveals the nature and level of opposition Paul was to encounter in his ministry. This can be seen in Acts 9:15-16 where it says, "But the Lord said to him, "Go, for this man is a [deliberately] chosen instrument of Mine, to bear My name before the Gentiles and kings and the sons of Israel; for I will make clear to him how much he must suffer and endure for My name's sake."

So the Lord was simply saying to Paul, be ready for your ministry is not going to be a walk in the park. Based on 15th verse from the above scripture one could have mistakenly assumed that Paul was going to enter into different areas and meet kings and commoners, Jews and Gentiles and be welcomed with open arms; however, verse 16 provides clarity that he was to find opposition and suffer greatly for the Gospel.

The Apostle Paul moved from one place to another to preach and teach the Gospel, and he faced all forms of verbal and physical attacks. When one reads his own narration of some of the things he went though, these may sound like a trailer from a horror movie, let us see 2 Corinthians 11:23-27 and it reads: "Are they ministers of Christ? - I speak as a fool - I am more: in labors more abundant, in stripes above measure, in prisons more frequently, in deaths often. From the Jews five times I received forty stripes minus one. Three times I was beaten with rods; once I was stoned; three times I was shipwrecked; a night and a day I have been in the deep; in journeys often, in perils of waters, in perils of robbers, in perils of my own countrymen, in perils of the Gentiles, in perils in the city, in perils in the wilderness, in perils in the sea, in perils among false brethren; in weariness and toil, in sleeplessness often, in hunger and thirst, in fastings often, in cold and nakedness." Paul was chosen and assigned by God to a great move of bringing the Gospel to people who either did not know it or were hell-bent on rejecting him, hence this move brought him great opposition.

One of the reasons Paul's ministry was opposed so greatly is because it was ushering the Kingdom of God and transforming lives; and those who were benefiting from the ignorance of the people were opposed to this sharing of knowledge that was going to free the people from their evil grip. In the midst of all that persecution and opposition, Paul continued to plant churches in various areas with fellow labourers of Christ, and he continued to write prolifically, even from prison cells, and fulfilled his mandate. He said he had been poured out as a sacrifice for the Gospel.

If your great move involves a great sacrifice to help free others in any form or shape, expect an onslaught of opposition, because some people may be benefiting from the helplessness of the people, and your move is disrupting their nefarious profit-making schemes. Paul stayed the course and kept moving irrespective of the storms of opposition, that is why he speaks in this manner towards the end of his assignment on earth,

2 Timothy 4:7 "I have fought the good fight, I have finished the race, I have kept the faith." Let us all always keep in our hearts what the Bible reminds us in Romans 8:31. It says, "What then shall we say to these things? If God is for us, who can be against us?" Even against great opposition keep moving when it is time.

When your move is backed by God, He is able to suspend the laws of nature and science in order to ensure the success of your move.

This section reveals clearly that the greater the movement, the greater the resistance or opposition; it is for this same reason that when a stone is thrown into a river it causes the ripple movement of the water, and the movement of the water confirms this, and the bigger the stone, the larger and longer lasting are the ripples. It is perhaps important to pause and remember that God is above and in control of the natural and scientific worlds. He commanded the waters to be gathered in the sea; he stopped time in order to allow Joshua to defeat the enemy; He parted the Red Sea; Jesus rebuked the storm and walked on water; God also caused darkness to fall on the land when Christ gave up His spirit on the cross, in the middle of the day. When your move is backed by God, He is able to suspend the laws of nature and science in order to ensure the success of your move.

CHAPTER SEVEN

HOW TO GET YOUR MOVE ON!

"If you can't fly then run, if you can't run then walk, if you can't walk then crawl, but whatever you do you have to keep moving forward."- Martin Luther King Jr

---

The journey throughout this book from the first page to the end of Chapter 6 was meant to demonstrate to you and me that life and motion cannot be separated, the same can be said about death and stagnation. There is sufficient evidence that if you do not get yourself unstuck, it is unlikely that your life will get any better. As humans, we all desire better lives and great achievements, however we know what they say about wishes, they are not horses that can just be ridden by anyone. To make a change in our circumstances and to get closer to an imagined glorious future, we need to get ready to get our move on. There are key elements that need to be considered in order to make a successful move. Let us see how we can get our move on.

◆ DECIDE ON YOUR MOVE

Indecision is the enemy of movement. When a person faces danger, they can stand frozen in indecision and suffer great harm; similarly, there have been many opportunities lost because of indecision. To be undecided is the same as being double-minded, and the Bible teaches us that a double-minded person should not expect to receive anything from God.

Indecision Is The Enemy Of Movement

Make a decision that you need to make a move. And to come to that conclusion there are a few signs that you need to consider and these include the following:

◆ Are you energised?

Life is energy, so when you are not energised it means it is likely that your environment is sucking the life out of you. If you have tried a few things to regain your energy levels, such as rest, exercise, studying, finding and pursuing new hobbies and interests, maybe you need to make the tough decision to get your move on.

◆ Which area of life is sapping your energy?

When you make the efforts to boost your energy levels, pay attention to each activity so you can zoom into the source of the problem. This will help you not to make a wrong decision based on inaccurate information, as this can backfire and cause more misery and stress.

◆ Desire

The Bible says God will give you the desires of your heart. If you have no desires, then you cannot initiate any meaningful move. You can only make a move based on what you desire to see, to feel, experience, or desire. It begins with a desire to live and be alive, when we have a desire to live and to be alive, we begin to appreciate life, and that life must keep moving to better levels. If you are in an undesirable place, you need a new desire to go to the desirable place.

You Need A New Desire To Go To The Desirable Place

◆ Take your time

Time is of the essence as we always learn, however this does not mean you must delay a decision indefinitely. To spend longer time than required on a decision is risky as it can pull you into the indecisiveness zone. Different decisions require different time periods to conclude. Remember that God works in times and seasons, that is why Genesis 8 : 22 teaches this when it says, "While the earth remains, seedtime and harvest, cold and heat, winter and summer, and day and night shall not cease."

◆ **Rationale**

Do not base your decision entirely on how you feel, but this does not suggest that you should ignore your feelings. However, ultimately rationality must guide the move so that it is not merely a reactionary spur of the moment action.

◆ **Consult**

It is important that you take a decision after consulting those who matter the most in your life. For example, before quitting your job or selling that business, what are your spouse or partner's thoughts on the decision you are contemplating to take. Be careful that a consultation does not turn into a session that blows out the candle of the decision that you are contemplating. If after consultation you decide not to proceed further, let that be based on the best advice and not on any other motive or motivation.

◆ Pray

God speaks, and He wants to be involved in all areas of our lives, it was not because He was bored that He counted the number of hairs on our heads, it is because of His love and utmost care for our well-being in all areas of our lives. Talk to God at various stages of your decision. We learned from David that before he made a decision to pursue the Amalekites he sought guidance from the Lord, and when God said to him it was a good and Godly idea, only then did he make a final decision. David had an idea about what he wanted to do, but he still left himself open to what God was going to say. Come to God with an open mind knowing that He may confirm your decision or He may advise to the contrary.

◆ Ownership

Once you have decided, own the decision and protect it; that is the only way to take it to the next phase. Be invested in your decision in one form or another. A prudent investor protects his investment and takes ownership of his decisions. If you do not take ownership, then such a decision may end up on the shelf, and from there it may be transferred to the dustbin like many others before.

◆ PLAN YOUR MOVE

You can stumble into failure often; accidental success on the other hand is rare. When you plan, you take into account what can go wrong, what can go right, what key considerations to take note of. A plan for your move should incorporate the following:

You Can Stumble Into Failure Often; Accidental Success On The Other Hand Is Rare.

◆ Vision

A plan that is not informed by a clear vision is a plan that is prone to failure. A plan that does not have an end in mind is likely to be derailed when the storms come. It is like a ship at sea and the captain is unsure of the intended destination, when the winds continue to batter it, it will go where the winds direct it. When the destination is clear, the captain will sail against the storms, and get to the destination, no matter how treacherous the voyage may be.

There are many definitions of vision; we can define vision as the ability to see beyond the natural, because it brings the future into the present, so a vision is a vivid colour picture of the planned and expected end. A clearly defined vision will provide us with a picture of what the successful completion of our move will look and feel like.

A vision must always be written down or recorded in some form, as Habakkuk 2:2 says, "Then the Lord answered me and said: "Write the vision and make it plain on tablets, that he may run who reads it." This reveals that it is difficult to run with a vision that you have not written down. A written or recorded vision demonstrates commitment and it forces us to be accountable to its fulfilment; secondly, when a vision is recorded, it is impossible to contaminate and alter it when tempests come. This vision will keep drawing us back on track.

A Vision Is A Vivid Colour Picture Of The Planned And Expected End

---

◆ Risks

A move is a risky undertaking. This is demonstrated by a child who is learning to walk, taking tentative steps, falling, and going at it again. The risk of falling is ever present, but the desire and excitement to walk always supersedes the risk of falling, hence the child keeps trying until she gets it. It is the same when we make a move, we must be aware that there will be risks; however, we must not dismiss those risks, nor should we use the potential risks as an excuse to hinder our move.

We must identify, evaluate, and assess potential risks with the intention of creating the appropriate risk responses. There will always be risks that we can mitigate, avoid and some may even have to be accepted. The decision on how to respond to the risks should be based on a sound risk analysis. If you think it is too risky to go out into the streets, you may still die of hunger in your bed, so risk analysis is not to encourage stagnation. We saw the four leprous men in chapter 7 of the book of 2 Kings. They were willing to step forward and risk their lives, but instead of premature death, they found abundance and were also able to deliver and preserve the remnant of the Israelites who were held hostage within the city walls.

Risk Analysis Is Not To Encourage Stagnation

Sometimes a move may look perilous; however, if you get to a point where it is more dangerous or costlier to remain stuck, maybe just step forward, your life might just be dependent on that one step. Although it looked like a death and death decision or what is known as a zero-sum game, the decision to remain stagnant or to move was a life and death decision for the leprous men, and the result was life (for the leprous men) and life (for the Israelites).

Like the leprous men, often your move will preserve other lives, destinies that you were not even aware of, so do not take any move lightly, as its impact, and implications can be far-reaching and even outlive you. There were possibly many other leprous men in the vicinity and outskirts of the city, however there is no mention of them in the Bible. The four leprous men who made a move are immortalised in the Bible and history, because they dared to move.

Your Life Might Just Be Dependent On That One Step

When the Apostle Paul was travelling and preaching the Gospel and planting churches, he was continually assessing the risks and responding to them accordingly, at one point his life was at risk, and the only escape for him was to be lowered down a window in a basket. It was not a pretty escape, but the level of risk required action that was out of the ordinary. Jesus Christ was nearly captured and killed before the appointed time, He recognised the risk and escaped from imminent danger.

It is therefore unwise to ignore risks, just because you feel so strongly about the move does not mean that you must throw all caution to the wind.

◆ **Count the Cost**

If a move is cheap, the results thereof may be insignificant; on the other hand, a move can become too costly. Some moves do not cost money, yet they can cost relationships, opportunities, market share, and career prospects. In the Bible, we see Jesus Christ teaching about counting the cost, in Luke 14:28 he asks, "For which of you, intending to build a tower, does not sit down first and count the cost, whether he has enough to finish it?"

Counting the cost includes ascertaining what resources you will need for your move, and these should include financial and non-financial resources. There may be a move that you intend to make, but this requires a certain skill that you currently do not have. You have to decide whether you will acquire this first and delay the move or outsource the skill, and if so at what cost.

A move that you make without counting the cost can become too costly to maintain or sustain, and often we will hear comments such as "the move was done prematurely", purely because the cost was not accounted for while the move was being planned, if the move was indeed planned. That is why Jacob had to compare the costs of continuing to live in Laban's house and that of leaving and returning to his hometown; he deduced that remaining stuck was too costly.

A cost that you should avoid is that of your health and peace. If a move will cost you your health or peace, even both, you may need to reconsider as the costs of these is too high a price, no matter how great and promising that move may appear to be.

◆ Pen the Plan

The final part of planning is to write the plan down. This is different to writing a vision because a vision is a bigger picture view of the puzzle, while a written plan deals with the individual pieces that are required to complete the puzzle. A proper house requires a detailed plan prior to construction; the same applies for a great move.

A plan that is written down ensures that there is correct resourcing, focus and directed effort at each stage of the move. The plan also provides key milestones as well as decision points along the journey of completing a move.

When Joseph interpreted the dream by Pharaoh about the impending seven years of plenty, and the subsequent seven of famine, he provided a plan on how each of the periods were going to be dealt with. It is safe to say this plan was written down, otherwise it would have been very difficult to stay on track, especially in times of abundance. That is why the harvest was able to be split correctly between the quantities that were to be consumed, what was to be stored for the long term, and what food products were to be produced in each year during the times of bumper harvests. Similarly, during the famine, the plan was used to determine how much was to be consumed and what volumes were to be sold to generate income. If there was no plan, Egypt would have probably run out food before the famine was over.

Get God To Have The Final Signoff On Your Plan

The plan must be easy to read and follow, and it must indicate key reflection points, so that reviews and adjustments can take place at the correct intervals. The plan must ultimately be fit for purpose, for example, a plan for a career change move is different from a plan to move out of debt. Do not kill a mosquito with a machine gun, neither bring a knife to a gunfight.

Lastly, get God to have the final signoff on your plan, it is advisable to do this from the outset, that is why Proverbs 16:3

teaches us thus, "Commit your works to the Lord [submit and trust them to Him], and your plans will succeed [if you respond to His will and guidance]." If God does not approve the plan, it is unlikely that He will protect it; He is a faithful God, He safeguards what He has approved.

You Must Not Make A Move To Prove A Point

◆ MOVE WITH INTENT

Accidents happen, and some accidents can push you towards your destiny; this however, is the exception rather than the norm. A move has to be intentional, especially if the aim is for the move to be successful. Other synonyms for intention are aim, goal, reason, or rationale.

Intention determines motive and motivation; these two words are not the same, though they are often used interchangeably, and we look briefly at these:

Motive

This answers the question why you are making a move and why you think the move is necessary. There are many reasons why some moves end in tears, but one of the most common is wrong motive. For example, you must not make a move to prove a point, do not make it to test the waters, do not make it as an act of revenge, do not make it as a form of rebellion, and it must not be impulsive. All these are examples; there are many others of reactionary motives.

The intention of any meaningful move should be to advance oneself, to advance a good cause, to address a problem, to form new partnerships, to use underutilised or untapped skills and abilities, to explore new opportunities; all these are proactive motives, as they are forward looking. David did not make the move against Goliath because he wanted to become king of Israel; he did it because he could not allow one man to disrespect and terrorise the people of God and get away with it. King Solomon, the son of King David did not ask for wealth, so that he could live lavishly and enjoy the trappings of power, instead he asked for wisdom to rule correctly. Motive is a matter of the heart, which manifests through the approach that is crafted by the mind. David was made king because his motive was pure; Solomon became the wise king, but because of his sincerity of motive, God added wealth, fame, and influence.

Motivation

Motive is reason, whereas motivation is what fuels the reason or motive, it is the inspiration, or the incentive. Motivation breeds resilience, tenacity, persistence, and perseverance.

Motivation provides the stimulus to press on even when days are dark, and friends are in very short supply. Many people commence with a great move but they are unable to see it through to completion due to lack of motivation. Motivation forces us to break through the barrier called comfort zone, because we recognise that great opportunities lie beyond the familiar.

Motivation, like happiness, is built from within. There are external stimuli that can serve as a source of motivation, however these must enter the mind and heart, and ignite the fire within and sustain it for the course. Jesus Christ faced an excruciating journey to the cross and we see it in how hard He prayed in Gethsemane where He even says these words in prayer as found in Matthew 26:39b "...My Father, if possible, let this cup pass from me! Yet not what I will, but what you will." He endured death on the cross because His motivation was to fulfil the Word of God and bring salvation to mankind, and this was the reason why He was able to override His own will for that of the Father.

Great Opportunities Lie Beyond The Familiar

The right motive and motivation will ensure that a move is intentional and it can therefore be sustained, especially in times of trials, tests, and tribulations. Intention forces us to check the reason why a move is being made, and the importance and validity of this reason.

◆ MOVE FOR IMPACT

There are two areas of impact, internal and external. So, a move must have an impact either on the mover or on their external environment. Some moves will impact both the person and their surroundings. Impact can also be constructive or destructive. The impact of an earthquake is not the same as the impact of a gentle rainfall, yet both do make an impact on the earth. The earthquake can cause death, while the water from the rain sustains life. If a move achieves great results and the mover is celebrated and showered with accolades, this can boost confidence and self-esteem, leading to improvement in self-worth and general well- being. If a move backfires and ends in disaster, this may kill the morale of the mover leading to a self-deprecating attitude, and this may cause them to abandon their dreams and passion for life. Let us explore the concept of internal and external impact a bit below:

◆ **External Impact**

Amove can have an impact on the external environment. This environment can be a geographical region, a natural environment, an industry, an organisation, or even a community. A great move will invariably have an impact on some of the environments that we just highlighted. If your move is to launch a new social media platform, the impact of this can be felt and seen in various areas, for example, the impact can be within the social media industry itself, in the business solutions environment, in education, and employment creation. In addition, it can even lead to an amendment of or introduction of new legislation, this move can even create new markets and stimulate investment.

◆ **Internal Impact**

This is impact on a personal level. In his song titled: “Man in the Mirror”, Michael Jackson once sang these words “if you wanna make the world a better place, take a look at yourself, and make that change”. The most impactful move is that which affects the movers themselves. When you are a timid and shy teenager, and decide to make a bold move to join the debating team at school, this move can backfire when you become a laughing stock for your lack of confidence and eloquence of speech. On the contrary, if this move helps improve your speech and assertiveness, this can be the catalyst for a love for speaking and presenting, and this can have a positive impact on self-image and motivation, and you can use it to soar to great heights.

The Most Impactful Move Is That Which Affects The Movers Themselves

---

To have a positive impact on self is dependent on the habits that we develop and nurture. Some bad habits can creep on us while we are unaware, but once we identify them and their potential negative impact, we should make a choice and change course. The prodigal son in the Bible had begun to settle into a habit of eating with pigs, and this was becoming his new normal. He had to break this pattern and rethink his current path, and choose between stagnation and progress. However, once he came to himself he made a move to break free from the habit of normalising an abnormal and subhuman existence.

There was a young man who had a father who loved education and strongly believed in the power of reading. The father encouraged the son to read widely, and to the chagrin of the boy, the father would often make him read and explain what he had read. In what appeared like a situation of adding salt to the wound or fuel to the fire, there was an elderly family aunt, who worked Emakhisini (a domestic worker for White families), and she would bring volumes of old books for the young man. This act of forethought by the aunt caused great delight to the father and equal displeasure on the lad. As time went by, the young man gained confidence in his reading and narration of the written text, and he began to enjoy reading. This young man got into a habit and routine of reading more than five books in three months, and this developed into a lifelong love for the written word.

Today the lad has grown into a man and he has started writing to contribute to what he loves. All this happened because a good habit was triggered, nurtured, and developed, and long after his life people would continue to read what was written by someone who loved to read. In your current transition point in life, you need to practice habits that are advancing you to where you desire to go next; remember that we are “the sum of our habits”.

Practice Habits That Are Advancing You To Where You Desire To Go Next

---

◆ Measures of Positive Impact

Impact can only be truly measured after the move. A positive impact is inspirational, and it provides a launching pad for self and others when they want to make impactful moves. We have seen how the great moves of people like Martin Luther King Jr, Madam C.J Walker, Franklin D. Roosevelt, and many others continue to affect our thinking, as well as inspire and shape the moves that we continue to make many years after they departed from this earth.

Abraham made a move that was impactful to an extent that he has descendants that are not of his biological lineage, because they look up to his walk with God. Moses's move to be concerned with the plight of the Hebrews made an impact on himself. He was able to make a very difficult choice of leaving the comfort of Pharaoh's palace where he was raised as a prince. His move entailed standing on the side of truth with the Hebrews who were in bondage at the time. Although he started in self-doubt, he listened to God and made a move back to Egypt where he was called by God to deliver the Hebrews from slavery.

He trained Joshua, Caleb and their contemporaries on how they were to possess the Promised Land and to observe God's commands. Therefore, what began as a personal move, which had an internal impact on Moses, ended up impacting the

Hebrews and many generations to come. The impact of Moses's move is seen in that he continues to be used as an example of how to move with God, even in the midst of great uncertainty, as well as how to hear from Him and obey His words even in the midst of the noise around you.

The patriarchs, judges, kings, prophets, and apostles in the Bible have left an impact on how to move in the power of God, to bring the good news, which is the Gospel of Jesus Christ, even to hostile environments. They became a demonstration of what it means to be sold out to a cause so that we can all learn that we should never approach any move half-heartedly. Their writings, as inspired by the Holy Spirit, have been included in the Bible cannon and we are beneficiaries of all the correction, guidance, encouragement, and nourishment that come from their contribution to the holy scriptures.

A Great Move In Its Nature Will Involve The Help And Support From Others

---

Assess the impact your move will have on you and those around you, your positive impact will inspire others to pursue their moves with the right attitude. Great external impact will always feature in history books, while great internal impact will create the passion, zeal, confidence, and creativity for the next move. The following quote by George Washington Carver demonstrates the power of impact; it says, "When you do the common things in life in an uncommon way, you will command the attention of the world." It does not matter how great or small the move is; if you do it uniquely, it will still make an impact. There is a need to ensure though that the impact of your move is positive, both internally and externally. An all-in approach to any move will result in a widely felt impact.

◆ MOVE IN HUMILITY

A humble heart is one that is able to receive correction without taking offence as part of the package. A humble spirit is teachable, and learning is best facilitated and it is most beneficial to a humble person.

It is seldom that a move can be a one-man show; a great move in its nature will involve the help and support from others. Some of the help and support will come to you unsolicited, but in many instances, the help and support will have to be requested, and without humility, it is not possible to ask for help. When David and his men were hungry and there was no food in sight, he humbly went into the temple to beg for bread from the priests, and as a result, he and his men were sustained and preserved. If he was proud he would have had a false sense of entitlement, especially since he was innocent and unfairly marked by king Saul for death, yet he did not fall into self-importance and pride.

The Apostle Paul talks about the importance of humility, in 1 Corinthians 12:7 where it says, “And lest I should be exalted above measure by the abundance of the revelations, a thorn in the flesh was given to me, a messenger of Satan to me, lest I be exalted above measure.” To be exalted above measure is to walk in pride and arrogance, so Paul was humbled by God, so that he could be useful in God’s hands, when we move in humility, we become like soft clay in the Potter’s hands, and God is able to mould us according to His purpose.

Humility Will Allow You To Make An Unglamorous Move Because You Know That It Fits In With

---

The Bigger Plan

Humility is pleasing unto God; that is why the Bible says God resists the proud, but He gives grace to the humble. Arrogance and pride are repulsive to many people, and these are able to shut doors for your next move. When you move in humility, you will not burn bridges because some of these bridges will be your only way to cross over to another level or dimension.

God will always give grace to a humble heart, so that you are never without help, guidance, and support. Humility will allow you to make an unglamorous move because you know that it fits in with the bigger plan. That is why a humble person is able to do a "lowly work" in order to gain experience or fund his or her next great move. To serve also requires great humility, and many were identified and promoted to greatness because of how humbly they served. Ruth's life is a great example of this; she was willing to humble herself and glean in Boaz's farm in order to serve Naomi and with the passage of time, she was the wife of Boaz and owner of the same field from which she used to glean.

Learn From Christ And Move In Humility

The greatest demonstration of humility is the Lord Jesus Christ, who the Bible says humbled himself even to death on the cross. The Bible says, "Humble yourself by the sight of the Lord and He will lift you up", and we see that God gave Christ the name above every other name in heaven, on earth and underneath the earth. Learn from Christ and move in humility; many will not see you rising but they will be surprised to see you at the top.

◆ MOVE FOR PURPOSE

There are many definitions of purpose, some call it the grand or master plan, some call it the heart's highest desire, others call it the entire reason for being alive, and others call it that one thing that you do joyfully even if you do not get paid for it. It is clear from various definitions that purpose gives meaning to life, and its fulfilment provides the truest and grandest sense of achievement. True purpose is usually greater than self and it has a multi-generational impact, so true purpose leaves behind a legacy for those who follow.

One mistake one should avoid at all cost is to sit and wait until they discover their purpose, or it drops miraculously on their lap. Purpose is normally discovered on a journey, and often that journey would have appeared to be headed nowhere. When Jacob stole the blessing and ran away from his brother Esau, it appeared as though he was going to spend the rest of his life as a fugitive, yet his steps were continually headed towards his destiny and purpose. It was through all the trials and difficulties that he went through in Laban's house that he realised that the blessing of the Lord was upon his life. It was ultimately this knowledge that emboldened him to wrestle with the angel of God until he was blessed and ushered into his purpose. He fulfilled the purpose for his life when he became

Israel and a father of the nation named after him, his legacy continues.

True Purpose Is Usually Greater Than Self

When God called Moses to make a move to free the Hebrews from slavery, he found him busy shepherding Jethro's sheep, and he was found by the mountainside in the pastures. There he saw the miracle of the burning bush that was not consumed, and God spoke to him, and redirected him to his purpose of bringing out the Hebrews from their bondage in Egypt. Paul encountered the Lord while he was on a crusade to arrest and persecute Christians, and God redirected him to his purpose, which was to preach the Gospel to the Gentiles and usher them into the Kingdom of God. Jesus Christ found the disciples while they were occupied with some assignment or another, and He redirected those he found fishing to be fishers of men, that is why Peter could preach and immediately thereafter call 3000 souls to Christ at one go.

We Should Never Approach Any Move Half-Heartedly

Jesus Christ had to assist his earthly father Joseph in the carpentry trade, before moving into His purpose which God had preordained before the creation of the universe; His purpose was to provide salvation and reconcile mankind with God.

Let God find you walking, so that He can merely redirect your steps, because it is easier to turn a car that is moving than one that is parked with the engine switched off. Every person's purpose is preordained and predesigned by God, even before they are born, and we are reminded of this in Jeremiah 1:5 when God says to the then young man, "Before I formed you in the womb I knew you, before you were born I set you apart; I appointed you as a prophet to the nations." Pursuing purpose starts where you are and demands that you use what you have, and God will continue to work things out for your good. In Psalm 37:23, we learn that "The steps of a good man are ordered by the Lord, and He delights in his way." When David was out in the field with the sheep and a lion snatched one of the lambs, and he went after it, slayed it, and rescued the lamb; he did not know at the time that this was preparing him for his purpose to become a courageous warrior king of Israel. It is important to run your own race, whether you have discovered purpose or not as yet, stay in your lane to stay sane! When you seek God, in that process He will reveal your purpose. A purposeful move is a move that is aligned with the will of God for your life.

◆ MOVE BY FAITH

Faith has never failed; and faith will never fail. Hebrews 11:1 provides the best definition of faith and it says, "Now faith is the substance of things hoped for, the evidence of things not seen." So, faith is both substance and evidence; substance is something that can be felt or touched, and evidence is something that is visible, so faith pulls things from the invisible realm into the physical realm.

Let God Find You Walking, So That He Can Merely Redirect Your Steps

---

It was by faith that Abraham believed that at 100 years of age and Sarah's wife at 90 they were going to have their son Isaac. It was by faith that Rahab, the prostitute, hid the Hebrews spies when they came to scout Jericho, and she and her family were spared when the city was destroyed. It was by faith that Mary believed that she would bear the Son Jesus Christ, even while she was still a virgin. It was by faith that when Paul's ship was wrecked while he was on his journey to Rome, he told the owners of the ship that no one was going to die.

It was by faith that Gideon went to battle with only 300 men and God gave them victory over a 120 000-men strong army. It was by faith that Elijah prayed for rain and it came pouring down. It was by faith that while Peter was in jail, the believers gathered to pray overnight and God sent an angel to release him from jail. It was by faith that Paul and Silas worshipped and praised God while they were in prison and God sent an earthquake to break open the prison doors. With faith, nothing is impossible.

Let God Find You Walking, So That He Can Merely Redirect Your Steps

---

Move in faith, knowing that God has angels, including in human form, who have been assigned you on your journey. The faith must be based on the knowledge that God has made grace available to help us in all areas where we require help. It is reported that each time Washington Carver needed a new invention, he would go into his study or laboratory and close the door and ask God for a new idea, and each time God would pour down brilliant ideas into his heart, and just like that, a new invention was born. Those who have faith should not suffer from costly trial and error moves that can breed stress, frustration, and fatigue.

The Bible says the just shall walk by faith and not by sight, that is why when the twelve spies went to scout out Jericho, ten of them brought back a negative report that was based on what they saw. They were afraid of the giants in the land, and they saw themselves as grasshoppers in the sight of those giants. Joshua and Caleb walked by faith, they saw by faith the land of promise, flowing with milk and honey, and the size of the giants was for them confirmation, that indeed there was good milk and honey in that land. By faith, they believed that the promise from God that they were to possess the land was based on the faithfulness of God. Some moves will bring you against giants in your company, region, industry, country or even in the world, but fear not, God is faithful, if the move is from Him, He has also made a way where there was no way, keep moving by faith.

With Faith, Nothing Is Impossible

A move of faith is always focused on the future because you understand that God moves you from glory to glory and your best years must always be ahead of you. The Hebrews who kept yearning for the "good old days" of Egypt failed to enter the Promised Land, the same thing happened to Lot's wife, after God had sent an angel to rescue them from Sodom and

Gomorrah and they were out of the city she looked back and she was turned into a pillar of salt. Jesus Christ warns us that anyone who puts the plow to the ground and looks back (focus on their past) is not fit for the kingdom. The Apostle Paul reminds us that we are to forget the things that are behind and press on forward; and it is only through faith that we are able to press forward on our move because we know that our feet will not step into a place that our faith has not visited beforehand.

A faith-filled move has a guarantee of success, it does not matter how many twists and turns one may encounter on the way, faith will bring you safely to your destination. The Bible says without faith it is impossible to please God, and this reveals that with faith in God, He will make the impossible possible because what is impossible with man is indeed possible with God. Move in faith, and by faith in God!

Move In Faith, And By Faith In God!

CONCLUSION

Stagnation is death, and we should never expect life in a place of death. If you are stuck, make up your mind that you do not belong there. Identify the move that will transcend you from death to life, plan that move and go for it. Your move will impact and inspire others, and remind them that they must never settle for any place lower than their God ordained destiny and purpose. You were not created for stagnation and failure, so refuse to stay in stagnation.

Isaiah 55:12 says, "For you shall go out in joy and be led forth in peace; the mountains and the hills before you shall break forth into singing, and all the trees of the field shall clap their hands." This is your portion, so get unstuck, choose life, and get your move on!

References:

www.ancient.eu
www.biblestudy.org
www.insight.org
www.theologyofwork.org
www.history.com
www.dailysabah.com
www.worldbank.org
www.stlouisfed.org
www.oecdobserver.org
www.fanack.com
www.sahistory.org.za
www.whitehouse.gov
www.biography.com
www.nobelprize.org
www.nelsonmandela.org
www.aerospace.org
www.interestingengineering.com
www.britannica.com
www.blacklivesmatter.com
www.globalchristianity.org
www.grc.nasa.gov www.phys.org
www.oxfordreference.com
Concise Oxford English Dictionary

Kotler, P. and Keller, K.L. 2009. A Framework for Marketing Management.

Lynch, R. 2012. Strategic Management

Mabuela, J.L. 2015. The 12 Success Factors.

Meyer, J. 2007. Battlefield of the Mind

Morris, P.W.G, and Pinto, K.K. 2007. Project, Program & Portfolio Management

Motshitela, P.S. 2015. Signature Vision

Mullins, L.J. 2002. Management and Organisational Behaviour.

Munroe, M. 2006. The Principles and Power of Vision

Thompson, A.A. and Strickland, A.J. 2003. Strategic Management.

Various articles and publications

www.ingramcontent.com/pod-product-compliance
Lightning Source LLC
LaVergne TN
LVHW091144080826
845145LV00008B/2246

* 9 7 8 1 9 9 0 9 6 1 4 5 8 *